A+ Complete Lab Manual

Third Edition

A+® Complete Lab Manual
Third Edition

Donald R. Evans

Scott Johnson

San Francisco • London

Associate Publisher: Neil Edde
Acquisitions Editor: Elizabeth Hurley Peterson
Developmental Editor: Colleen Wheeler Strand
Production Editor: Susan Berge
Technical Editor: Warren Wyrostek
Copyeditor: Tiffany Taylor
Compositor/Graphic Illustrator: Judy Fung
CD Coordinator: Dan Mummert
CD Technician: Kevin Ly
Proofreaders: Monique van den Berg, Emily Hsuan, Darcey Maurer, Laurie O'Connell, Nancy Riddiough
Indexer: Ted Laux
Book Designers: Bill Gibson, Judy Fung
Cover Designer: Archer Design
Cover Photographer: Colin Paterson, PhotoDisc

How to Become CompTIA Certified:

This training material can help you prepare for and pass a related CompTIA certification exam or exams. In order to achieve CompTIA certification, you must register for and pass a CompTIA certification exam or exams.

In order to become CompTIA certified, you must:

(1) Select a certification exam provider. For more information please visit http://www.comptia.org/certification/test_locations.htm.

(2) Register for and schedule a time to take the CompTIA certification exam(s) at a convenient location.

(3) Read and sign the Candidate Agreement, which will be presented at the time of the exam(s). The text of the Candidate Agreement can be found at www.comptia.org/certification.

(4) Take and pass the CompTIA certification exam(s).

For more information about CompTIA's certifications, such as their industry acceptance, benefits, or program news, please visit www.comptia.org/certification.

CompTIA is a non-profit information technology (IT) trade association. CompTIA's certifications are designed by subject matter experts from across the IT industry. Each CompTIA certification is vendor-neutral, covers multiple technologies, and requires demonstration of skills and knowledge widely sought after by the IT industry.

To contact CompTIA with any questions or comments:
Please call + 1 630 268 1818
questions@comptia.org

Contents at a Glance

Contents

Introduction

This lab manual is a companion workbook for Sybex's *A+ Complete Study Guide* by David Groth (Sybex, 2003), which is designed to prepare technicians for the A+ Certification Test. This lab manual is loaded with dozens of real-life, hands-on PC repair activities. Successfully completing the labs in this manual will reinforce complex concepts presented to you in the Study Guide by providing practical hands-on applications of the concepts.

Regardless of your method of training for the A+ certification, this book will complement your study regime. For best results, read the appropriate chapter suggested at the beginning of each chapter, perform the related labs, and review the A+ written lab questions in the text. Each chapter in this book has a note explaining which chapter of the Study Guide to refer to for more information. If you are using this lab manual by itself in a classroom setting, the scenarios and instruction for each lab contain enough information that labs can be completed on their own.

Each lab is set up in a straightforward, easy-to-follow pattern. Every lab in the manual provides you with the following:

- Objectives to be accomplished

- A list of hardware needed in the lab

- A list of software needed in the lab

- An introduction to the lab

- Step-by-step procedures for the lab

- A lab report for observations and information

These labs emphasize the major concepts covered in the *A+ Complete Study Guide*. Each chapter of this book contains a reading suggestion for specific chapters in the Study Guide. The labs are broken down into sections with step-by-step instructions. Windows command line and DOS commands along with the proper syntax are shown throughout the book. Some labs (those without operating systems identified in their title) may be performed on either a DOS system or a Windows system.

> In this book, DOS and command-line characters that you *key* (type at the keyboard) are shown in boldface after the prompt, and the prompt and the path are shown in standard print. DOS is not case-sensitive, but in this book commands to be typed are shown in uppercase and the prompt is shown in mixed case. The following example shows that the Directory (DIR) command is to be typed. This command will be executed in the Windows directory of drive C: C:\Windows>**DIR**.

> The topics covered in this book follow the same pattern as those in the *A+ Complete Study Guide*, 3rd edition.

What You'll Need

You'll need a few hardware and software items to perform the labs in this book.

Required Equipment

A 486 (or newer), Windows 95 or better computer with a CD-ROM drive, at least 8MB of RAM, and a 200MB IDE hard drive will permit you to do most of the labs in this book. To do every lab in this book, the following equipment or its equivalent is required: a 133MHz Pentium with 32MB of RAM, a 1GB hard drive, a VGA monitor, a CD-ROM drive, and a 3½-inch floppy drive. A less valuable 486 (or newer) computer can be used for many of the hardware labs to save wear and tear on your more valuable computers. Computers that are used for the hardware labs may not be operational at the end of each lab session.

 Some exercises are repeated using different versions of Windows, from 9x to XP.

If computers are to be used by more than one group of students, removable drive trays can reduce interference between students. You'll also find that some labs require further specific equipment:

- A mouse and keyboard
- IDE interface hard drive
- IDE interface CD-ROM drive
- Miscellaneous cables and hardware fittings
- Sound card
- InPort mouse card or jumper-configured adapter card
- Printer
- Network interface card and cable for each computer that will be attached to the network

Required Software

In order to perform every lab, you need the following software (however, many of the exercises have variations for each version of Windows):

- DOS 6.x
- Windows 95
- Windows 98
- Windows 2000
- Windows NT 4.0

- Windows XP
- Microsoft mouse driver
- Sound card driver
- CD-ROM driver
- Printer driver

Required Tools and Supplies

Finally, there are a few tools and safety items you should have available:

- Antistatic wrist strap
- Antistatic mat
- Flat-blade screwdriver
- Phillips screwdriver
- Long-nose pliers
- Blank floppy disks
- Multimeter

   The following list of goodies is recommended for the labs in this manual, not to mention that they are very useful to have on hand in your toolkit:

- Band-Aids
- Flashlight
- Hemostat
- Keeper tube
- Magnifying glass
- Tweezers

Safety, Safety, and More Safety

If you are ready to disassemble a PC or even begin minor repairs, then undoubtedly you've read a number of reminders concerning safety. If you are sitting in a classroom, then it is likely that your instructor has covered safety in detail as well. To ensure that you're safe and that your equipment isn't damaged during any of these labs, let's recap some general guidelines.

Use Your Anti-ESD Equipment

ESD charges can cause problems such as making a computer hang or reboot. Electrostatic discharge (ESD) happens when two objects of dissimilar charge come in contact with one another.

The two objects exchange electrons in order to standardize the electrostatic charge between them. This charge can, and often does, damage electronic components.

To use an ESD strap, you attach one end to an earth ground (typically the ground pin on an extension cord) and wrap the other end around your wrist. This strap grounds your body and keeps it at a zero charge.

 WARNING   There is only one situation in which you should not wear an ESD strap. If you wear one while working on the inside of a monitor, you increase the chance of getting a lethal shock.

Because many of the devices you'll be working with are extremely sensitive to ESD damage, you should also have an ESD mat in addition to an ESD strap. The mat drains away excess charge from any item that comes in contact with it. ESD mats are also sold as mouse/keyboard pads to prevent ESD charges from interfering with the operation of the computer. Many wrist straps can be connected to the mat, so you and any equipment in contact with the mat are at the same electrical potential, thereby eliminating ESD.

Finally, remember to have plenty of antistatic bags on hand to protect sensitive electronic devices from stray static charges during your lab work. If you can't get to an electronics supply store before you begin the work in this book, you can reuse any of the bags from previous computer or component purchases.

Power Supply

Do not take the issue of safety and electricity lightly. Remember that computers not only *use* electricity, they *store* electrical charge after they're turned off. In addition, the computer's processor and various parts of the printer run at extremely high temperatures, and you can get burned if you try to handle them immediately after they've been in operation. When you open your computer to inspect or replace parts (as you will with most repairs), be sure to turn off the machine before you begin.

 WARNING   Other than the power supply, one of the most dangerous components to try to repair is the monitor, or cathode ray tube (CRT). In fact, we recommend that you *do not* try to repair monitors. Reserve these repairs for trained electrical repair professionals.

Common Sense

When you're repairing a PC, do not leave it unattended. Someone could walk into the room and inadvertently bump the machine, causing failure. Worse, they could step on pieces that may be lying around and get hurt. Most of the components have cords. Although there usually isn't much danger associated with tripping, it still poses some concern. Keep your workspace tidy by keeping cords tucked and unused tools out of the way.

Always remember to handle parts and electronic components correctly. Be careful to avoid direct contact with connectors and expansion slots, or anything that could be damaged from ESD.

It is also not a good idea to work on a PC alone. If you're injured, someone should be around to help if necessary. Finally, if you're fatigued, you may find it difficult to concentrate and focus on what you are doing. There are real safety measures related to repairing PCs, so the most important thing to remember is to pay close attention to what you are doing.

Chapter

1

PC Architecture

LABS YOU WILL PERFORM IN THIS CHAPTER:

✓ **Lab 1.1: Safely Examining the Computer**

The inside of a PC is made up of modules and submodules, with the motherboard providing connection points for all the other modules. The processor (brain of the computer) performs mathematical and logic functions. The BIOS (basic input/output system) contains software for the POST (power on self test), the boot process, and hardware configuration information. The system memory (RAM) is usually located on the motherboard and is loaded with the operating system during the boot process. The CMOS (battery-powered memory) chip, which retains the setup information needed for the boot process, is on the motherboard as well. A variety of storage devices such as the hard disk and floppy drive are also mounted inside the computer case. Some of these items can easily be visually identified, whereas others are easier to identify through software.

In this chapter, you will learn how to identify these components and do so in an environment that is safe for both you and the equipment.

For more information on PC architecture, see Chapter 1 of David Groth's *A+ Complete Study Guide* (Sybex, 2003).

Lab 1.1: Safely Examining the Computer

In this lab, you'll examine the internal and external components of the computer. But before you open a computer, you must consider the safety issues. Practicing proper electrical safety procedures when you work with a computer's hardware is essential. Safety precautions protect the computer, as well as the technician.

Upon completion of this lab, you will be able to:

- Practice electrical safety while working on computers
- Protect the computer from electrostatic discharge (ESD) damage
- Identify and document the common external computer connections
- Identify the motherboard type
- Locate and identify storage devices
- Use the operating system to identify components

Specific Safety Issues

The safety of the technician and the computer must be considered when a computer is being repaired or updated.

Safety of the Technician

Electrical shock hazards can be greatly reduced by unplugging all cables from the computer before you open the computer case.

The power outlet is the most likely source of a deadly electrical shock. The 120 volts from the power outlet are sufficient to cause death. The power supply should not be plugged into a wall outlet unless it is first attached to the motherboard. The power supply itself should never be opened. Its components can store a charge that can result in a serious shock or worse.

Untrained personnel should never open a monitor, because its components may store dangerous electrical charges for long periods after the power has been turned off.

Safety of the Equipment

For the safety of the computer, do not rely on your memory. Take notes, draw diagrams, and mark cables as you remove them. Without this information, reassembly becomes a guessing game.

Static electricity can damage a computer that is being serviced. Anyone who opens the computer case should unplug all external cables, wear an antistatic wrist strap, and use an antistatic mat as a work surface.

WARNING You should never wear an antistatic wrist strap when the computer is attached to a power source, because the antistatic wrist strap conducts electricity.

The antistatic wrist strap is worn on the wrist and attached to a bare metallic part of the computer; this equalizes the electrical charge between the technician and the computer. Without this connection, as little as 30 volts of static electricity can destroy computer components. Sometimes, components damaged by electrostatic discharge (ESD) do not fail immediately but fail after a few hours of use. If an antistatic wrist strap is not available, you can reduce the ESD hazard by frequently touching a bare metal part of the computer. This frequent touching of a bare metal surface tends to equalize the static charge, but this method is not as effective as using an antistatic strap.

You should place an antistatic mat on the work area to prevent static damage to parts after they are removed from the computer case. An antistatic bag can be used as an antistatic mat if an antistatic mat is not available.

Identifying Computer Components

The components of a computer can be divided into external and internal categories.

External Connections

The external ports provide connections for peripheral devices. By examining these ports, the technician can gain insight as to the system's capabilities. (See Figure 1.1.)

FIGURE 1.1   External ports

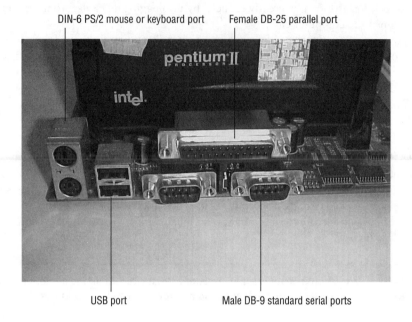

DIN-6 PS/2 mouse or keyboard port   Female DB-25 parallel port

USB port   Male DB-9 standard serial ports

Internal Components

Internal components may be identified physically or by using the operating system to examine the system components. In reality a combination of identification methods works best, because some components may be damaged in the removal and installation process.

Figure 1.2 shows typical PC components for a desktop computer. The interconnecting cables are missing, so the internal parts are more visible in the figure than in real life.

FIGURE 1.2   Typical PC components

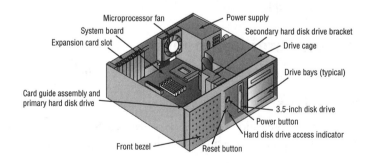

Microprocessor fan   Power supply
System board   Secondary hard disk drive bracket
Expansion card slot   Drive cage
                        Drive bays (typical)
Card guide assembly and
primary hard disk drive
                        3.5-inch disk drive
                    Power button
                    Hard disk drive access indicator
Front bezel   Reset button

The motherboard contains all circuitry necessary for components and devices to communicate with each other. This board provides sockets for all the components and peripherals used by the computer. (See Figure 1.3.)

FIGURE 1.3   Components on a motherboard

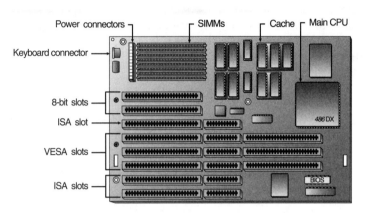

Three basic form factors (AT, ATX, and NLX) are currently used for the motherboard construction. An AT motherboard has power only when the computer is turned on, whereas an ATX motherboard, whose power switch is connected directly to the motherboard, has power in some circuits any time the power cable is connected to a power outlet. (In general, it is not a good idea to work on computers when they are connected to the power outlet unless you are performing a voltage test.) An easy way to determine the motherboard type is to examine the motherboard power connector. The AT motherboard has a single row of pins sticking up from the power connector; the ATX motherboard has a rectangular socket with two rows of pins. The ATX power connector is keyed so the connector fits only one way; the AT power connector has two plugs that fit the socket, and they can easily be reversed. Reversing these connectors will damage the motherboard. The quick and easy way to make sure that the connectors are correct is to place the black wire to the black wire.

The NLX (low-profile) motherboard has a riser card that contains the expansion bus slots. Several manufactures make NLX computers, but the boards are proprietary and usually do not fit into computer cases from other manufacturers.

The processor is usually covered by a heatsink and fan and should not be disturbed. The processor is generally identified during the boot process. If you press the Pause/Break key at the right time, the screen freezes, and you can record the information. The BIOS chip is usually exposed and often has useful information printed on its label, such as the BIOS manufacturer's name and the processor it supports.

The computer stores information in the memory while you are working; however, when the computer is shut down, the information in RAM is lost. Computers' long-term storage uses media that does not require continuous power; the media could be memory sticks, CD-ROM drives, floppy drives, or hard drives. CD-ROM drives, floppy drives, and hard drives are usually mounted in the drive cage.

Set Up

For this lab exercise, you will need a working PC with any Windows operating system installed.

Exercises

This lab shows how to safely open a computer case and identify computer hardware components.

Identifying External Connections

1. Boot the computer to verify that it is bootable.

2. Shut down the computer and turn off the power to all peripherals.

3. Sketch the back of the computer, showing where each cable is attached.

4. Disconnect all external computer cables. As you disconnect them, add the function of each port to the sketch, and note the port configuration. (For example, you will probably find a Video Graphics Array, female, 15-pin, compact D connector on your computer, and PS/2 connectors for the keyboard and mouse.)

Removing the Cover

1. With all external cables disconnected from the computer, remove the cover screws that are usually found around the back edge of the case.

If an antistatic mat is available, place it on the work surface and place the computer on top of the antistatic mat. Equalize the electrical charge between the work surface and the computer by connecting them together. A wire with alligator clips on each end is often used to connect the mat to a bare-metal part of the computer.

2. Pull off the back edge the computer cover and lift up the cover. Do not remove the cover until you have your ESD equipment ready.

3. As soon as the cover is removed, put on the antistatic wrist strap to protect the computer from ESD.

Place the antistatic wrist strap around your wrist with the metal portion of the wrist strap touching bare skin. Connect the wrist strap's alligator clip to a bare-metal part of the computer case. Doing so equalizes the electrical charge between you and the computer. As little as 30 volts of static electricity can damage computer parts. Do not wear an antistatic strap while working inside a computer that is attached to the power cable.

4. With the cover off and ESD controls in use, examine the parts inside the computer, but *do not disconnect any internal parts or cables*. You may gently move wires aside to obtain better views of the motherboard, but you must not disconnect any wires.

5. Identify the motherboard form factor. Use the power connector to distinguish between AT and ATX motherboards.

6. If you can, locate the BIOS chip and record the manufacturer's name (such as Award AMI).

_____

7. List the storage devices found. You can do little more than count the number of devices and examine both the external and internal portions of the devices to determine their type. If a drive is not visible from outside the case, it is probably a hard drive.

_____

_____

8. Replace the computer case and reconnect all external cables.

9. Boot the computer. If it boots successfully, you know you have everything connected as it should be.

10. In a Windows 98 system, obtain the processor type and memory size with the following sequence after the computer has booted to the Desktop:

    Start ➢ Programs ➢ Accessories ➢ System Tools ➢ System Information

    Record the processor type and total (RAM) memory.

_____

A Windows XP system gives better information than other Windows versions, but the path to the System folder is different. In a Windows XP system, use the following:

> Start ➤ Control Panel ➤ Performance and Maintenance ➤ System ➤ General Tab

11. In Windows 98, click the plus sign in front of the Components option. In the Components tree, select Storage and then list the drives that are displayed.

_____

_____

In Windows XP, use the following to see the drives.

> Start ➤ Control Panel ➤ Administrative Tools ➤ Computer Management. In Computer Management under Storage, click Disk Management.

12. Record the hard-drive size (capacity) and free space as expressed in the System Information window.

_____

Lab Report 1.1

1. What is the best method of preventing ESD damage?

_____

_____

_____

_____

2. What type of connector is used for a parallel port?

_____

_____

3. What is the best method of avoiding electrical shock?

_____

_____

_____

_____

4. What type of connector is used for a VGA or SVGA monitor?

_____

_____

_____

_____

5. Identify the external connections in the diagram.

Answers to Lab Report 1.1

1. Wear the ESD strap and have it connected to a bare-metal part of the case any time the case is open and external cables are removed.

2. The parallel port uses a 25-pin female D connector.

3. Do not work inside a computer if external cables are connected, and do not open the computer monitor unless you have special training about monitors.

4. A 15-pin compact D connector is used for VGA and SVGA monitor ports.

5. Answer:

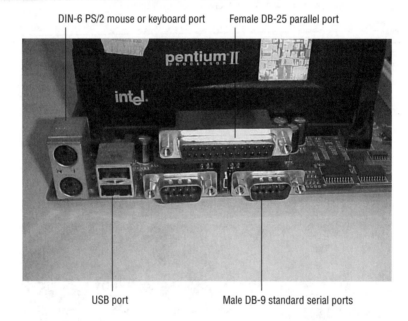

DIN-6 PS/2 mouse or keyboard port   Female DB-25 parallel port

USB port   Male DB-9 standard serial ports

Chapter

2

Motherboards, CPUs, and RAM

LABS YOU WILL PERFORM IN THIS CHAPTER:

✓ **Lab 2.1: PC Motherboard Architecture**

✓ **Lab 2.2: PC Bus Architecture**

✓ **Lab 2.3: Optimizing DOS Memory**

✓ **Lab 2.4: Examining Windows 98 Memory Areas**

✓ **Lab 2.5: Examining Windows 2000/XP Memory Areas**

This chapter will guide you further in recognizing the major components of a PC: the CPU, RAM, and peripherals. We will begin with the motherboard architecture. You need to become familiar with where the CPU and RAM are located. Additionally, you need to know where and how peripheral devices connect to the motherboard. Several categories of peripheral devices have developed—everything from the original 8-bit ISA devices and slots to special ports for video cards and 32-bit PCI devices and slots.

The physical memory (RAM) is one of the primary components of the motherboard, and each operating system uses RAM differently. This chapter will cover how to check the memory from DOS, Windows 98, Windows 2000, and Windows XP.

For more information, see Chapters 1 and 2 of David Groth's *A+ Complete Study Guide* (Sybex, 2003).

Lab 2.1: PC Motherboard Architecture

The A+ exam requires you to be able to recognize many components that make up a PC. It all starts with the kind of motherboard, or *form factor*, the PC uses. We will cover how to recognize the motherboard form factors and how to identify the components on the motherboard. The primary topic of this section is how to recognize the many different memory packages. Later in the chapter, we will discuss how the operating systems use memory.

Let's go over some of the concepts you need to understand:

AT Form Factor   The AT form factor was designed by IBM. Its distinguishing features include the position of the keyboard plug and the type of power connectors (see Figure 2.1). Problems with the AT form factor include its large size and the lack of other external connectors.

Baby AT Form Factor   The baby AT form factor was introduced as technology improved and the demand for smaller computers increased. Essentially, the baby AT is the same as the full AT, but it's significantly smaller. It uses the same power connectors, and its only external connector is the keyboard plug.

ATX Form Factor   The ATX form factor incorporates all the external connectors we are familiar with today (see Figure 2.2). The power connector has been changed to a P1 connector, which simplifies the connection and provides continual power to the motherboard. The size of the ATX motherboard remains small, like the baby AT.

FIGURE 2.1 AT form factor

Power supply
connector

AT style
keyboard
plug

COM and LPT
ports require
ribbon cables

CPU

Expansion slots
parallel to
wide edge

FIGURE 2.2 ATX form factor

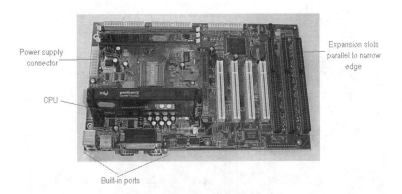

Power supply
connector

CPU

Built-in ports

Expansion slots
parallel to narrow
edge

CMOS/BIOS The Complementary Metal Oxide Semiconductor (CMOS) chip houses a set of programming instructions called the Basic Input/Output System (BIOS). Because this is the only function of the CMOS chip, the names are almost interchangeable. The BIOS runs the programs that allow the computer's devices to communicate with the CPU. The CMOS setup routine allows you to interface with these programs to configure the devices in the computer.

Flash ROM   This fills the same function as the CMOS. The main difference is that you can reprogram the chip without removing it. Flash ROM gives you the flexibility to update the BIOS when new technologies emerge. It has become the primary chip used today. Visually, it is difficult to distinguish between the older CMOS and today's Flash ROM chips.

CPU Socket   Luckily, the exam doesn't expect you to be able to visually recognize the differences between the many CPU sockets that have been created over the years for all the different processors. It does, however, require that you be able to identify which processors are associated with the different sockets. Visually, you have to be able to identify a Zero Insertion Force (ZIF) socket and a Slot 1 socket, which uses the Single Edge Processor (SEP), on the motherboard.

RAM Bank   Random access memory (RAM) is the working memory of the computer. It has undergone many improvements over the years. The most visible of these improvements is in the packaging and the way memory banks are populated. Memory was first packaged with DIPPs; the latest packaging uses memory sticks. The exam will ask questions that test your ability to recognize the different packages.

DIPP   Dual Inline Pin Packages (DIPPs) were the first generation of dynamic random access memory (DRAM). A DIPP consisted of a chip with two rows of pins that were pushed into the sockets on the motherboard (see Figure 2.3). The memory bank consisted of rows of DIPPs.

FIGURE 2.3   Dual Inline Pin Package (DIPP)

SIPP   Single Inline Pin Packages (SIPPs) simplified the installation of memory. Instead of installing multiple DIPPs to create a bank of memory, you could install sticks of memory (see Figure 2.4). Each bank consisted of two sticks; each stick had the DIPPs soldered to the stick. The motherboard had special sockets for the installation of the stick.

FIGURE 2.4   30-pin SIPP

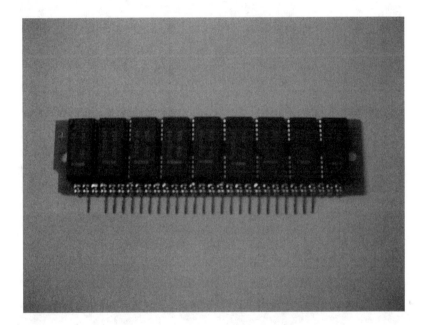

SIMM   30-pin Single Inline Memory Modules (SIMMs) were the next improvement in memory packaging (see Figure 2.5). The pins were removed to simplify installation. The number of sticks needed to create a bank varied based on the external data bus. The 16-bit data bus used two sticks, the 32-bit data bus used four sticks, and the 64-bit data bus used eight sticks per bank.

With the 32-bit data bus, 72-pin SIMMs grew in popularity (see Figure 2.6). The major improvement was that the sticks of memory were also 32 bits wide. This meant few sticks were needed to complete a data bank. Each stick of 72-pin SIMMs was the equivalent of four 30-pin SIMMs. The distinguishing factor was that the sticks were longer and had a notch in the center.

FIGURE 2.5 30-pin SIMM

FIGURE 2.6 72-pin SIMM

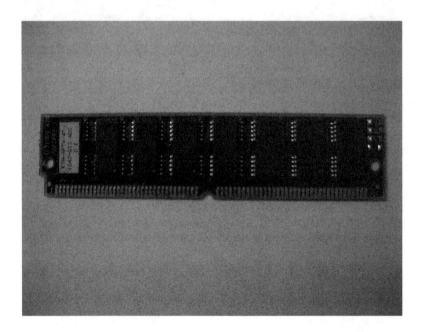

DIMM SIMMs were replaced by Dual Inline Memory Modules (DIMMs). The first DIMMs were nothing more than two SIMMs on the same stick. The number of pins increased to 168, and the data bus is 64 bits wide (see Figure 2.7). The physical characteristics now include two notches to make installation easier. This package is the current package for memory. All of the new types of memory—SDRAM, EDO, and DDR SDRAM—are packaged the same.

FIGURE 2.7   168-pin DIMM

SoDIMM Laptops had their own problems with memory packaging. The solution for laptops was the introduction of the Small Outline DIMM (SoDIMM), which makes accessing and installing RAM a simple process (see Figure 2.8).

Upon completion of this lab, you will be able to:

- Recognize the motherboard form factors.
- Identify the components of the motherboard.
- Be familiar with the various memory packages.

FIGURE 2.8   SO-DIMM

Set Up

For this lab, you will need a working computer.

Exercise

In this lab you will open a PC and document its components, such as the location and type of the CPU, RAM, and BIOS.

1. Take the cover off your computer. Examine the motherboard.

2. Make a drawing of the motherboard and its components.

3. Label each component on the drawing.

4. Record the name of the BIOS:

_____

5. Record the type of processor:

_____

6. Record the type of RAM and the RAM package:

_____

Lab Report 2.1

1. What is the function of the BIOS?

_____

_____

_____

_____

2. What are some common ways to access the CMOS setup program?

_____

_____

_____

_____

3. What is the difference between CMOS and Flash ROM?

_____

_____

_____

_____

4. What are the different RAM packages?

_____

_____

_____

_____

Lab 2.2: PC Bus Architecture

A *bus* is a set of signal pathways that allow information and signals to travel inside or outside the computer. Computers have internal buses (inside the microprocessor) and external buses (outside the microprocessor). In this lab, we will explore external buses and expansion slots for peripheral devices. The expansion bus (slot) provides power (+5 volts, +12 volts, and ground), the data bus allows for information exchange, the address bus provides access to memory, and the control bus is used for clock signals, IRQ signals, and so on.

First let's consider some of these features:

Interrupt   The interrupt request (IRQ) is a bus feature that permits a device to signal the processor to get the processor's immediate attention. An interrupt indicates that an event requiring the processor's attention has occurred, causing the processor to suspend and save its current activity and then branch to an interrupt service routine. This service routine processes the interrupt (whether it was generated by a keystroke or a mouse click) and, when it's complete, returns control to the suspended process. Ideally, each device has its own IRQ number.

DMA Channel   Direct Memory Access (DMA) is a bus feature that allows devices to bypass the processor and write their information directly into main memory. Each type of bus has a different number of DMA channels available. If two devices are assigned the same DMA channel, neither device will work.

I/O Address   The processor treats each device as a memory location and sends information to that address or reads information from that address. This I/O address is unique for each device that communicates with the processor.

Memory Address   A memory address is assigned to each device and gives the memory location of the required subroutine the processor needs to service the device. These subroutines are usually found in the ROM BIOS or other ROM chips.

Clock Signal   Each computer has a metronome-like clock signal measured in megahertz (MHz) or gigahertz (GHz). The internal click determines the processor speed, and the bus clock determines the bus speed. Because different processors run at different speeds, motherboards usually provide for changing the clock speed to match the processor in use.

Bus Mastering   Bus mastering permits some expansion buses to take control of the external data bus. Bus mastering is much faster than DMA.

Chipset   The chipset is a set of chips that work in conjunction with the processor to control peripherals. The chipset usually includes LSI (large-scale integration) chips such as SiS, AMD, or OPTi that control many of the motherboard features. (See Figure 2.9.)

FIGURE 2.9   Motherboard with an OPTi chipset

Expansion Buses   Several types of motherboard expansion buses (expansion slots) have been developed over the years. A technician needs to be able to identify the various expansion slots so the correct expansion cards are specified during ordering. You also need to know about the expansion buses in order to make intelligent decisions about upgrading systems. The PCI and AGP bus expansion slots are found on newer computers, but you may encounter the other slots:

- The 8-bit ISA (Industry Standard Architecture) bus operates at 4.7MHz. Windows XP supports few ISA cards. The 16-bit ISA bus operates at 8MHz (10MHz in turbo). The 16-bit ISA bus was introduced by IBM in 1984 and is found on some Pentium motherboards. (See Figure 2.10.)

FIGURE 2.10   ISA 8-bit and 16-bit expansion slots

- The 32-bit EISA (Extended ISA) was little used and is not found in newer computers.
- The 16 or 32-bit MCA (Micro Channel Architecture) is electrically and physically incompatible with other buses. IBM developed it for the PS/2 computer; it provides for bus mastering and software configuration.
- The 32-bit VESA (Video Electronics Standards Association) was a 16-bit ISA bus with an additional higher density connector. The VESA (also called a local bus or VL bus) operated at 33MHz and used bus mastering.
- Currently the 32-bit PCI (Peripheral Component Interconnect) bus, which operates at 66MHz, dominates the industry. The PCI expansion bus supports bus mastering and is available in a 64-bit version that is about five inches long; the 32-bit PCI expansion bus is only about three inches long. (See Figure 2.11.)

FIGURE 2.11   PCI bus connector

- Most new computers use the 32-bit or 64-bit AGP (Accelerated Graphics Port) for their video expansion cards. The AGP operates at 66MHz and comes in several versions with throughputs up to 1Gbps. The expansion slot looks much like the PCI expansion slot but is offset on the motherboard and is usually brown, whereas the PCI slot is usually white. (See Figure 2.12.)

FIGURE 2.12   An AGP slot on a motherboard

Upon completion of this lab, you will be able to:

- Identify the chipset
- Identify motherboard expansion slots and bus types
- Explain bus features

Set Up

For this exercise, you will need a PC motherboard that can be examined.

Exercise

1. Examine a motherboard.
2. Make a drawing of the motherboard and its bus expansion slots.

3. Label each bus expansion slot with its bus type, bus width in bits, and bus speed in MHz.
4. List the buses found that support bus mastering.

_____

5. Record the name of the chipset.

_____

Lab Report 2.2

1. What is the function of a motherboard expansion slot?

_____

_____

_____

_____

2. What is a bus?

_____

_____

_____

_____

3. What is the function of the chipset?

_____

_____

_____

_____

4. Why is the AGP use for the video port in most new computers?

_____

_____

_____

_____

Lab 2.3: Optimizing DOS Memory

Logical memory is the way physical memory is seen by the operating system. The MS-DOS memory map shows the first 640KB of RAM as the user (conventional) area and the rest of the first megabyte of RAM as reserved for the computer's needs. The user area is the problem area for DOS users because DOS uses some of the conventional memory as you load applications or add new hardware drivers. As conventional memory is used, programs that have been running may report insufficient memory when they are next executed. The usual solution to this problem is to optimize memory.

You can optimize DOS memory usage manually by modifying the AUTOEXEC.BAT and CONFIG.SYS files or using the MEMMAKER utility. DOS experts can do a better job of optimizing memory than the MEMMAKER utility, but the number of DOS experts is in decline. For most situations, running MEMMAKER yields satisfactory results.

Upon completion of this lab, you will be able to:

- Determine memory usage in a DOS system

- Optimize memory in a DOS system

Set Up

For this lab, you will need a working computer with DOS 6.x installed.

Exercises

In this lab, you will examine DOS memory utilization. You will also free up additional conventional memory by optimizing DOS memory with the MEMMAKER utility.

Examining DOS Memory Usage

To examine DOS memory usage,

1. Boot the computer to drive C:.

2. Run the MEM utility to display the current memory utilization:

   C:\>**MEM**

   Record the memory information from the MEM utility in Table 2.1.

TABLE 2.1   Memory Information

Memory Type	Total	Used	Free
Conventional	_____KB	_____KB	_____KB
Upper	_____KB	_____KB	_____KB
Reserved	_____KB	_____KB	_____KB
Extended (XMS)	_____KB	_____KB	_____KB
Total memory	_____KB	_____KB	_____KB
Total under 1MB	_____KB	_____KB	_____KB
Largest executable-program size	_____KB		
Largest free upper-memory block	_____KB		

Optimizing DOS System Memory with the *MEMMAKER* Utility

To optimize DOS system memory with the *MEMMAKER* utility,

1. Enter the following command to optimize the DOS memory with the MEMMAKER utility:

   C:\>**MEMMAKER**

   Accept the default conditions as the program runs.

2. If the computer fails during the MEMMAKER utility, warm-boot the computer, run MEMMAKER again, and choose Try Again with Conservative Settings.

3. If the computer is unable to boot after MEMMAKER runs, boot to a DOS utility disk and enter the following command to undo the optimization:

   C:\>**MEMMAKER /UNDO**

4. After MEMMAKER has finished optimizing the system's memory and reboots the computer, run the MEM utility again:

   C:\>**MEM**

Record the memory information from the MEM utility in Table 2.2.

TABLE 2.2   After-Optimization Memory Information

Memory Type	Total	Used	Free
Conventional	_____KB	_____KB	_____KB
Upper	_____KB	_____KB	_____KB
Reserved	_____KB	_____KB	_____KB
Extended (XMS)	_____KB	_____KB	_____KB
Total memory	_____KB	_____KB	_____KB
Total under 1MB	_____KB	_____KB	_____KB
Largest executable-program size	_____KB		
Largest free upper-memory block	_____KB		

5. Compare the conventional memory usage listed in Table 2.1 with that listed in Table 2.2. If the Free amounts in Table 2.2 are greater than those in Table 2.1, the optimization was successful.

Lab Report 2.3

1. What indicates that you need to optimize DOS memory?

_____

_____

_____

_____

2. What is the function of the MEMMAKER utility?

_____

_____

_____

_____

3. What types of memory are nonvolatile?

_____

_____

_____

_____

4. What is the function of the MEM utility?

_____

_____

_____

_____

Lab 2.4: Examining Windows 98 Memory Areas

Before you begin this lab, you should understand the concepts of *logical memory* and *reserved memory*. Logical memory is the way physical memory is seen by the operating system. Windows does a good job of managing system memory. The MS-DOS memory map shows the first 640KB of RAM as the user (conventional) area and the rest of the first megabyte of RAM as reserved for the computer's needs. Windows uses memory above 1MB (expanded memory) and memory below 640KB (conventional memory) as if it were one bank of memory.

The memory area between conventional (640KB) and expanded (1024KB) is reserved for system components. This area is known as the Upper Memory Block or high memory. This area of RAM is reserved for the system board BIOS, video, and peripheral devices.

Upon completion of this lab, you will be able to:

- Use Device Manager to examine memory
- Use the System Information folder to examine memory

Set Up

For this lab, you will need a working computer with Windows 98 installed.

Exercises

In this lab, you will examine memory areas in a Windows 98 system. Windows 98 does a good job of managing system memory; however, you will have problems if the system has insufficient memory.

Using Device Manager to Examine Memory Resources

To use Device Manager to examine memory resources,

1. Use the following sequence to open the System Properties dialog box:

    Start ➤ Settings ➤ Control Panel ➤ System

2. Select the General tab in the System Properties dialog box and record the RAM:

    _____

3. Select the Device Manager tab in the System Properties dialog box and then select Computer. Click Properties and then click the Input/Output radio button. Record the communications port (COM 1) I/O address:

    _____

4. Click the Memory radio button and record the system board BIOS address (Settings):

    _____

5. Close all windows.

Using the System Information Dialog Box to Examine Memory Resources

To use the System Information dialog box to examine memory resources,

1. Use the following to open the system information dialog box:

    Start ➤ Programs ➤ Accessories ➤ System Tools ➤ System Information

2. In the System Information dialog box, click the plus sign by Hardware Resources to open the hardware tree. In the hardware tree, click I/O and record the I/O address (I/O Range) used by COM 1:

    _____

3. In the hardware tree, click Memory and record the memory addresses used by the system board BIOS:

    _____

4. In the System Information dialog box, click System Information and record the percentage of system resources that are free:

    _____

    If less than 30 percent of system resources are free, the computer may not function properly if you open an additional program.

5. Without closing the System Information dialog box, open a program such as Paint and then minimize the program:

    Start ➤ Programs ➤ Accessories ➤ Paint

6. Select System Information in the System Information dialog box, click View, and then click Refresh. Record the percentage of system resources that are free. The difference in the amount of resources listed in step 4 and step 6 are the resources used by the program you just opened.

    _____

Lab Report 2.4

1.   What is the function of the I/O address?

_____

_____

_____

_____

2.   What is the advantage of DDR SDRAM over SDRAM?

_____

_____

_____

_____

3.   Why are some peripherals assigned an area of memory addresses?

_____

_____

_____

_____

4.   What is the path to the System Information dialog box for Windows 2000?

_____

_____

_____

_____

Lab 2.5: Examining Windows 2000/XP Memory Areas

The Task Manager provides information about programs and processes running on your Windows 2000/XP computer. The following are categories of memory displayed by the Task Manager:

Total Physical Memory   Total physical memory is the total RAM installed in the computer.

Available Physical Memory   Available physical memory is the portion of installed RAM that is not allocated to a program or process.

Commit Charge   Commit charge is memory allocated to programs and processes. The Commit Charge may be larger than the total physical memory because it includes used virtual memory.

Kernel Memory   Kernel memory is memory used by the operating system.

Handles   The Handles value indicates the number of object handles (instructions handled).

Threads   Threads are objects that run program instructions. Threads allow more than one program instruction to be run at one time.

Processes   Process are tasks that are currently active.

System Cache   System cache is the current physical memory used to map pages of open files.

Paged Memory   Paged memory is memory used in the paging process. Paging is the process of moving infrequently used parts of a program from RAM to a storage medium.

Non-Paged Memory   Non-paged memory is operating system memory that is never paged to disk.

Upon completion of this lab, you will be able to:

- Use the System Information folder to examine memory
- Use the Task Manager to examine memory usage

Set Up

For this lab, you will need a working computer with Windows 2000/XP installed.

Exercises

In this lab, you will use the System Information dialog box and the Task Manager to examine memory usage in a Windows 2000/XP system.

Using the System Information Dialog Box to Examine Memory Resources

To use the System Information dialog box to examine memory resources,

1. Use the following sequence to open the System Information dialog box:

    Start ➤ All Programs ➤ Accessories ➤ System Tools ➤ System Information

2. Select the System Summary and record the following information:

    Total Physical Memory:

    _____

    Available Physical Memory:

    _____

    Total Virtual Memory:

    _____

    Available Virtual Memory:

    _____

    Page File Space:

    _____

3. In the System Information dialog box, click the plus sign by Hardware Resources to open the hardware tree. In the hardware tree, click I/O and record the I/O address (I/O Range) used by COM 1:

    _____

4. In the hardware tree, click Memory and record the memory addresses used by the system board:

    _____

5. In the hardware tree, click Conflicts/Sharing and list memory address that are shared:

_____

Using the Task Manager to Examine Memory

To use the Task Manager to examine memory,

1. To open the Task Manager, right-click the Taskbar and select Task Manager.

2. Click the Performance tab and record the following information:

CPU Usage:

_____

Paged Usage:

_____

Physical Memory Total:

_____

Physical Memory Available:

_____

Commit Charge Total:

_____

3. Without closing the Task Manager, use the following sequence to open the Paint program:

Start ➤ All Programs ➤ Accessories ➤ Paint

4. Without closing the Paint program, open Control Panel:

In Windows 2000:

Start ➤ Settings ➤ Control Panel

In Windows XP:

Start ➤ Control Panel

5. You should now have the Task Manager, the Paint program, and Control Panel running. Record the following information:

    CPU Usage:

    _____

    Paged Usage:

    _____

    Physical Memory Total:

    _____

    Physical Memory Available:

    _____

    Commit Charge Total:

    _____

6. When you compare the values from step 5 with the values from step 2, you should find that opening the two tasks caused an increase in resource usage. If the usage exceeds 70 percent, the computer is likely to have difficulty.

7. Click the Applications tab and record the displayed tasks:

    _____

8. Click the Processes tab and record the memory usage of the Paint program (MSPAINT.EXE):

    _____

Lab Report 2.5

1. What is Commit Charge?

_____

_____

_____

_____

2. What is kernel memory?

_____

_____

_____

_____

3. What is Physical memory?

_____

_____

_____

_____

4. What is the function of the Task Manager?

_____

_____

_____

_____

Answers to Lab Reports

Lab Report 2.1

1. The BIOS runs the programs that allow the computer's devices to communicate with the CPU.

2. The CMOS setup routine can be accessed in several different ways, depending on the brand. Some of the more common ways to start the routine are to press Del, F2, Ctrl+F1, or Ctrl+Alt+Esc. Most manufacturers tell you how to enter the CMOS setup as the computer is booting.

3. Flash ROM can be reprogrammed with the chip installed on the motherboard.

4. DIPPs, 30-pin SIPPs, 30-pin SIMMs, 72-pin SIMMs, and 168-pin DIMMs.

Lab Report 2.2

1. The motherboard expansion slot connects the computer bus to the expansion card.

2. A bus is a set of signal paths.

3. The chipset works in conjunction with the processor to control many motherboard functions.

4. The AGP slot provides faster video.

Lab Report 2.3

1. A DOS program refuses to run and reports insufficient memory.

2. MEMMAKER is used to optimize DOS memory in a DOS system.

3. ROM, PROM, and Flash RAM are nonvolatile.

4. The MEM utility displays memory information.

Lab Report 2.4

1. The CPU uses the I/O address to send information to a peripheral device.

2. DDR SDRAM transfers data two times for each clock cycle; SDRAM transfers data once per clock cycle. Therefore, DDR SDRAM is twice as fast.

3. This gives exclusive control of that area of memory to that device. A memory conflict is created if any other device tries to use the same memory area.

4. Start ➤ Programs ➤ Accessories ➤ System Tools ➤ System Information in Windows 2000.

Lab Report 2.5

1. Commit Charge is the total memory allocated to programs and processes.

2. Kernal memory is the memory used by the operating system.

3. Virtual memory is an area of the hard drive that is treated as if it were memory.

4. The function of the Task Manager is to display memory usage information.

Chapter 3

Disk Drive Storage

LABS YOU WILL PERFORM IN THIS CHAPTER:

- ✓ Lab 3.1 Replacing a Floppy Drive
- ✓ Lab 3.2 Replacing an IDE/ATA Hard Drive
- ✓ Lab 3.3 Replacing a SCSI Hard Drive

Disk drives were developed to create permanent storage for data. This was necessary because the data stored in memory is lost whenever the computer is shut down or loses power. The original form of permanent data storage for a PC was the floppy drive. Over the years we saw many improvements to the floppy that included a reduction in size and an increase in storage capacity.

The most common means for storing data in today's PC is the hard drive. The hard drive provides a medium for permanent storage that has become affordable, and the amount of data that can be stored is rising very rapidly.

A hard drive consists of one or more platters coated with magnetic medium. Each platter has read/write heads that float slightly above the platter. The heads read and write the data to the magnetic surface below. The heads are attached to an arm called the head actuator, which is controlled by a servomotor. The hard drive connects to the rest of the motherboard through an interface. The three most common interfaces used to connect a drive are Integrated Drive Electronics (IDE), Enhanced Integrated Drive Electronics (EIDE), and Small Computer Systems Interface (SCSI).

Although the floppy disk became a popular method for removable data storage, its storage capacity limits its functionality. Newer forms of removable media are being developed that include formats like Zip, Jaz, Kanguru, CD-ROM, and DVD. Removable media allow users to transfer data between computers easily and without having a network. The newer improvements have increased the reliability and longevity of the data stored.

This chapter will explore how to install floppy drives and hard drives. The labs will cover how to install both IDE/ATA and SCSI hard drives. You will find that over time you may need to upgrade your hard drive or install additional hard drives to increase the amount of data storage available in you computer. If you need to install other types of data storage, such as CD-ROMs, DVDs, or other removable media, the procedures are very similar to installing hard drives.

For more information, see Chapter 3 of David Groth's *A+ Complete Study Guide* (Sybex, 2003).

Lab 3.1: Replacing a Floppy Drive

The 5¼-inch floppy drive was part of the original PC. Most personal computers still have a floppy drive, although these days it is usually a 1.44MB 3½-inch drive.

Replacing a floppy disk drive in any computer involves opening the case—and that means you may lose the computer's CMOS disk drive settings. Without its CMOS data, the computer won't work, so you must be able to replace this data. Therefore, you need to make a record of this data before you begin the process of floppy-drive replacement.

Remember to practice standard ESD safety anytime you open the case. It's important!

Upon completion of this lab, you will be able to:

- Remove a floppy drive
- Install a floppy drive

Set Up

For this exercise, you will need a working computer with a floppy drive installed.

Exercises

In this lab, you'll run a CMOS setup and record the data. Then you'll work through the steps of removing any expansion cards in your path, removing the floppy drive, and reinstalling the floppy drive.

Removing a Floppy Drive

To remove a floppy drive,

1. Run the CMOS setup routine and record the drive data in the table provided:

You can access the CMOS setup routine several different ways, depending on the brand of BIOS. Some of the common ways to start the routine are to press Delete, F2, Ctrl+F1, or Ctrl+Alt+Esc. Most manufacturers tell you how to enter the CMOS setup as the computer is booting.

Drive	Physical Size	Capacity	
A:	_____	_____	
B:	_____	_____	

Drive	Cylinders	Heads	Sectors
C:	_____	_____	_____
D:	_____	_____	_____

2. Boot the computer, place a floppy disk in drive A:, right-click the drive A: icon in the My Computer window, and then click Explore to display the floppy disk's contents to verify that drive A: is operational.

3. Shut down the computer and turn off the power to all peripherals attached to the computer.

4. Open the computer case.

 As soon as the cover is removed, put on your antistatic wrist strap to protect the computer from ESD.

5. If any of the expansion cards are obstructing your access to the floppy drive, you need to remove them. *Important: Before you remove any expansion cards, prepare a sketch that shows where each expansion card goes in the motherboard expansion slots and where any cables or wires are connected to the expansion card.* On your sketch, note the pin 1 edge (the edge that has a stripe) on the cables and the colors of individual wires attached to the expansion card.

6. Once the sketch has been completed, disconnect any wires and cables connected to the expansion cards that are obstructing your access and remove the cards one at a time. To remove a card, remove the mounting screw, grasp the expansion card with both hands, and pull upward while gently rocking the board from front to back (see Figure 3.1).

FIGURE 3.1   Removing an expansion card

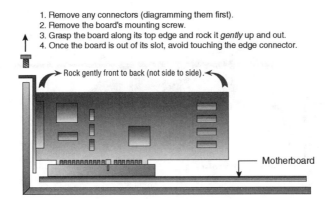

1. Remove any connectors (diagramming them first).
2. Remove the board's mounting screw.
3. Grasp the board along its top edge and rock it *gently* up and out.
4. Once the board is out of its slot, avoid touching the edge connector.

Rock gently front to back (not side to side).

Motherboard

7. As soon as the expansion card is out, place it on an antistatic mat to protect against ESD.

Any expansion cards that are removed must be reinstalled before you replace the computer cover.

8. The power cable plug on the floppy drive is keyed so it fits only one way, but the ribbon (data) cable can be accidentally reversed. To keep this from happening, note the pin 1 position of the floppy drive so you can later match it with the striped edge on the data cable when the drive is reinstalled. After you've done this, disconnect the ribbon (data) cable and power cable from the floppy drive. Note the pin 1 position to the controller on the motherboard and remove the floppy cable from the controller.

9. To remove the floppy drive from the computer, unbolt or release the floppy drive from the drive bay and pull the drive out of the front of the computer. You may have to remove the front panel to do this.

Installing a Floppy Drive

To install a floppy drive,

1. Slide the drive into the drive bay and fasten it in.

2. Attach the DC power connector to the drive.

3. Attach the ribbon (data) cable to the drive, with the striped edge of the ribbon cable on pin 1 of the floppy-drive plug. If this is the only floppy drive in the computer, it is drive A: and must be attached to a connector that is between the twisted wires and the end of the cable. If this is a second floppy drive, it is drive B:. Drive B: must be attached between the twist in the floppy-drive cable and the floppy-drive controller. (See Figure 3.2.)

FIGURE 3.2 A typical floppy cable

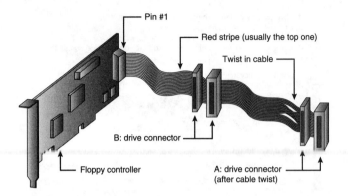

4. Attach the ribbon cable to the controller with the striped edge on the cable connected to pin 1 on the controller.

5. Using the sketch you made, reinstall all expansion cards that you removed. To install an expansion card, place the card in the same motherboard slot from which you removed it and press down firmly until the card is seated in the slot. Reconnect any cables or wires you disconnected from the card, and then replace the expansion card screw.

6. Replace the computer cover and connect all external cables.

7. Run the CMOS setup sequence. If the floppy drive indicated in the CMOS is incorrect for the new drive, select the type of drive you installed. When you exit CMOS setup, the computer will reboot, and the new settings will be loaded.

8. Boot the computer, place a floppy disk in drive A:, right-click the drive A: icon in the My Computer window, and then click Explore to display the floppy disk's contents to verify that drive A: is operational

9. If drive A: isn't working, check whether the floppy-drive light is always on. A floppy-drive light that is constantly on usually indicates that the data cable is upside down.

Lab Report 3.1

1. Where is drive A: attached to its data cable?

_____

_____

2. By what characteristic can you identify pin 1 on the ribbon cable?

_____

_____

3. What might be the problem if the floppy-drive light stays on but the drive does not function?

_____

_____

4. Where is drive B: attached to its data cable?

_____

_____

Lab 3.2: Replacing an IDE/ATA Hard Drive

The IDE specification was originally written in 1988. When it got accepted as an ANSI standard, it was renamed Advanced Technology Attachment (ATA). Although ATA is the official name, most technicians call it by its original name, IDE.

IDE provided an inexpensive interface for supporting storage devices like hard drives, tape devices, and CD-ROMs. The first IDE hard drives had a maximum capacity of 528MB. An enhanced version of IDE called EIDE or ATA-2 was released in 1996. This new standard allowed hard drives to reach a maximum capacity of 137GB. Later enhancements, known as ATA33, ATA66, and ATA100, increased storage capacity to a theoretical size of 144PB. The newer drives spin faster, allowing for increases in data transfer rates. These new drives rival the capacity and speed of its rival, SCSI devices.

Upon completion of this lab, you will be able to:

- Remove an IDE/ATA hard drive
- Install an IDE/ATA hard drive

Set Up

For this exercise, you will need a working computer with an IDE hard drive installed and a partitioned IDE hard drive that can be installed.

Exercises

In this lab, you will record the current hard-drive setup information, remove the hard drive, determine the hard-drive setup information for the drive to be installed, set the hard-drive jumpers, install the hard drive, and then configure the CMOS if the drive is not automatically detected. You can install the same hard drive or a different one. Any hard drive you install must be compatible with the BIOS of your computer and the operating system you are using.

Removing the Current Hard Drive

To remove the current hard drive,

1. Use the following space to record the CMOS settings for the current hard drive. Most hard drives manufactured in the last several years automatically detect the proper settings. Auto-detection has made setting the hard-drive type obsolete. Occasionally, however, you may have to use the User Type to enter the appropriate geometry. The geometry can be located on the case of the hard drive.

    Cylinders:

    _____

    Heads:

    _____

    Sectors:

    _____

2. Open the computer case.

WARNING   As soon as the cover is removed, put on your antistatic wrist strap to protect the computer from ESD.

3. If any of the expansion cards are obstructing your access to the hard drive, you need to remove them. *Important: Before you remove any expansion cards, prepare a sketch that shows where each expansion card goes in the motherboard expansion slots and where any cables or wires are connected to the expansion card.* On this sketch, note the pin 1 edge (the edge that has a stripe) on the cables and the colors of individual wires attached to the expansion card.

4. Once the sketch has been completed, disconnect the wires and cables that are connected to the expansion card, remove the mounting screw, grasp the expansion card with both hands, and pull upward while gently rocking the board from front to back (see Figure 3.1).

5. As soon as the expansion card is out, place it on an antistatic mat to protect against ESD.

Any expansion cards that are removed must be reinstalled before you replace the computer cover.

6. The power cable plug on the hard drive is keyed so it fits only one way, but the ribbon (data) cable can be accidentally reversed if it is not keyed. To keep this from happening, note the pin 1 position of the hard drive so you can later match it with the striped edge on the data cable when the drive is reinstalled. After you've done this, disconnect the data cable (ribbon cable) and power cable from the hard drive.

7. Physically remove the hard drive from the computer. Unbolt the hard drive from the drive bay and then remove the drive from the computer.

8. In another sketch, draw the hard-drive jumper block and show the current jumper settings.

The jumper settings should be master or single if this is the bootable drive. If the jumper settings do not match the installation, the drive will not function. Hard drive jumpers found in various locations on hard drives set the installation options.

If any hard-drive jumper is moved, the hard-drive configuration is changed. Sometimes it is very difficult to find documentation for jumper settings. Hard drives may be configured as *master, single, slave, or cable select*. The hard-drive configuration must match the drive's usage. The cable select status permits the computer to automatically select the master or slave status, but it requires a special hard-drive cable that is identified by a notch or hole in the cable.

Installing an IDE Hard Drive

To install an IDE hard drive,

1. Research the settings for the new hard drive and record the jumper and CMOS setup information in the space provided:

   Cylinders:

Heads:

_____

Sectors:

_____

 Newer hard drives have diagrams of their jumper blocks on their labels.

2. Set the jumpers on the new hard drive so they have the same function (master, slave, or cable select) as the drive you removed from the computer. The jumper blocks may be very different.

3. Install the new hard drive in the drive bay and attach the power cord to the hard drive. Place the drive into the drive bay and bolt it in place.

4. Attach the ribbon cable to the hard disk drive and the hard disk controller, with the striped edge of the ribbon cable on pin 1 of the plugs. On early hard drives and on most new hard drives, the drive that is attached to the end of the ribbon cable is drive C:. For some systems, the drive position on the ribbon cable does not matter.

5. Reassemble the computer (replace the expansion cards and the cover).

6. Start the CMOS setup sequence and make sure the settings match those of the new drive. Usually the hard drive is automatically detected; however, if the computer BIOS does not automatically detect the drive, you must set the heads, cylinders, and sectors manually. Sometimes a hard drive is detected with the wrong settings. The wrong settings may cause the hard drive to be installed with the wrong size specified.

7. Exit the CMOS setup. The computer will reboot.

8. Boot to a startup disk in drive A: and then attempt to access the drive you installed:

   A:\>C:

9. If you see the message *INVALID DRIVE SPECIFICATION*, the drive needs to be formatted. Use the FORMAT command to format the new drive:

   A:\>FORMAT C:

   When the format is complete, use the following command to access the hard drive:

   A:\>C:

10. If the C: prompt is displayed, the installation is a success.

Lab Report 3.2

1. What drive select jumper settings are available on a typical IDE hard drive?

_____

_____

_____

2. Which drive is usually installed as the master drive on the primary IDE interface?

_____

3. For a new hard drive, where are you likely to find the information needed to set up the CMOS?

_____

4. If the CMOS is set to auto-detect hard drives and the hard drive is detected with cylinders, heads, or sectors that are different from those listed on the hard drive label, what should you do?

_____

_____

Lab 3.3: Replacing a SCSI Hard Drive

SCSI (Small Computer Systems Interface) is an interface standard that supports a variety of internal and external peripheral devices. The most popular of the devices are hard drives, but SCSI also supports devices like printers and scanners. Since its inception, SCSI has undergone many improvements, each one increasing aspects of the standard, such as speed and number of supported devices.

The SCSI specification can be categorized into three official standards: SCSI-1, SCSI-2, and SCSI-3. The original SCSI-1 interface supports 5MBps transfer rate and supports up to 7 devices. SCSI-2 has several improvements and variations that include data transfer rates up to 20MBps and support of up to 15 devices. SCSI-3 also has multiple implementations that support data rates of up to 160MBps and support for up to 15 devices.

Unlike IDE devices, which usually have one jumper to select between master, slave, or cable select status, SCSI devices have three jumpers to set their ID number. These jumpers provide eight binary combinations from 000 to 111. The host adapter (SCSI controller) is usually device 7, whereas a bootable hard drive is usually device 0. Up to eight SCSI devices can be connected to the same SCSI-1 or SCSI narrow cable; the first last devices on the cable are terminated with a resistor bank. The terminating resistor bank can be physically inserted or removed, it can be electrically inserted or removed by a single jumper, or it can be set with software. SCSI devices can be connected as internal devices, external devices, or a combination of internal and external devices. See Figure 3.3 for an example of internal SCSI connections.

FIGURE 3.3   Cabling internal SCSI devices

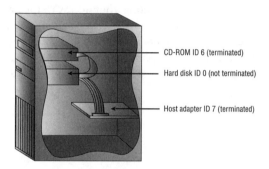

CD-ROM ID 6 (terminated)

Hard disk ID 0 (not terminated)

Host adapter ID 7 (terminated)

Internal SCSI devices usually use a 50-pin ribbon cable; there are several types of external SCSI cables. Consult the installation manual for your peripheral device for cabling instructions.

Upon completion of this lab, you will be able to:

▪ Remove a SCSI hard drive

▪ Install a SCSI hard drive

Set Up

For this exercise, you will need a partitioned SCSI hard drive to install and a computer with a working SCSI hard drive and SCSI controller installed. The computer's hard-drive size is limited by the system BIOS, the hard-disk SCSI controller, and the operating system in use. This installation assumes that the computer has a functioning SCSI adapter installed and configured.

Exercises

In this lab, you will record the current hard-drive setup information, remove the hard drive, determine the hard-drive setup information for the drive to be installed, set the hard-drive jumpers, install the hard drive, and check the SCSI configuration to see if the hard drive is configured. You can install the same hard drive or a different one. Any hard drive you install must be compatible with the BIOS of your computer, the SCSI controller, and the operating system you are using.

Removing the Current SCSI Hard Drive

To remove the current SCSI hard drive,

1. Boot to the CMOS and verify the CMOS hard-drive settings. The CMOS should indicate SCSI or NO DRIVE.

2. Open the computer case.

 As soon as the cover is removed, put on your antistatic wrist strap to protect the computer from ESD.

3. If any of the expansion cards are obstructing your access to the hard drive, you need to remove them. *Important: Before you remove any expansion cards, prepare a sketch that shows where each expansion card goes in the motherboard expansion slots and where any cables or wires are connected to the expansion card.* On your sketch, note the pin 1 edge (the edge that has a stripe) on the cables and the colors of individual wires attached to the expansion card.

4. Once the sketch has been completed, disconnect the wires and cables connected to the expansion card, remove the mounting screw, grasp the expansion card with both hands, and pull upward while gently rocking the board from front to back (see Figure 3.1).

5. As soon as the expansion card is out, place it on an antistatic mat to protect against ESD.

 Any expansion cards that are removed must be reinstalled before you replace the computer cover.

6. The power cable plug on the hard drive is keyed so it fits only one way, but the ribbon (data) cable can be accidentally reversed. To keep this from happening, note the pin 1 position of the hard drive so you can later match it with the striped edge on the data cable when the drive is reinstalled. After you've done this, disconnect the SCSI data cable (ribbon cable) and power cable from the hard drive.

7. Physically remove the hard drive from the computer.

8. In another sketch, draw the hard-drive jumper block and show the current jumper settings and terminating resistor. The jumper settings should be a binary number from 000 to 111. The boot hard drive is usually set to binary 0, which is indicated by no SCSI ID jumpers being set. The first and last devices on the cable are terminated with a resistor bank.

Installing a SCSI Hard Drive

To install a SCSI hard drive,

1. Verify the hard-drive CMOS settings. The CMOS should be set to SCSI or NO DRIVE.

 Newer hard drives have diagrams of their jumper blocks on their labels.

2. Set the jumpers on the new hard drive to have the same SCSI ID number as the drive you removed from the computer. Set the terminating resistor if it was set on the hard drive you removed.

3. Install the new hard drive in the drive bay and attach the power cord to the hard drive.

4. Attach the SCSI ribbon cable to the hard disk drive and the SCSI hard disk controller, with the striped edge of the ribbon cable on pin 1 of the plugs.

5. Reassemble the computer (replace the expansion cards and the cover).

6. Boot the computer and press Ctrl+A. You should see the message *Press Ctrl+A for SCSI Select*. The SCSI hard drive should appear in the SCSI scan.

7. Boot to a startup disk and access the hard drive:

   `A:\>C:`

8. If you see the message *INVALID DRIVE SPECIFICATION*, the drive needs to be formatted. Use the `Format` command to format this new drive:

   `A:\>FORMAT C:`

   When the format is complete, use the following command to access the hard drive:

   `A:\>C:`

9. If the computer shows a `C:` prompt, the installation was a success.

Lab Report 3.3

1. What is the binary number range for the SCSI device ID number?

   _____

2. Which SCSI devices must be terminated with a termination resistor?

   _____

3. What type of cable is used to connect an internal hard drive to the SCSI hard drive controller?

   _____

4. What SCSI ID is normally assigned to the bootable hard drive?

   _____

Answers to Lab Reports

Lab Report 3.1

1. Floppy drive A: is attached between the twist in the floppy-drive cable and the end of the floppy-drive cable.
2. The pin-1 edge of the floppy-drive cable is marked by a colored stripe.
3. The floppy-drive cable is probably installed upside down.
4. Floppy drive B: is attached between the twist in the floppy-drive cable and the floppy-drive controller.

Lab Report 3.2

1. Drive select jumpers let you choose between master, slave, or cable select.
2. The bootable hard drive is usually installed as the master hard drive on the primary IDE interface.
3. The hard-drive information for CMOS setup is usually found on the hard drive's label.
4. Manually set the hard-drive values in CMOS.

Lab Report 3.3

1. You can use SCSI ID numbers from binary 000 to binary 111.
2. The first and last devices connected to the SCSI chain must be terminated.
3. A 50-pin ribbon cable is usually used.
4. A bootable SCSI hard drive is usually assigned the ID number 000.

Chapter

4

Printers

LABS YOU WILL PERFORM IN THIS CHAPTER:

- ✓ Lab 4.1: Printers and Printer Interfaces
- ✓ Lab 4.2: Installing an Imaginary Printer in a Windows 98 System
- ✓ Lab 4.3: Installing an Imaginary Printer in a Windows XP System

At some point, most computer users need to print the information they have created and collected on their computer. In this chapter, we will go over some of the issues involved in attaching a printer to a computer.

Three major types of printers are used today. Laser printers are used for high-volume print applications, whereas the less expensive bubble-jet printers are used for small print volumes. Dot-matrix printers are used when an impact printer is needed—for instance, when working with multipart forms.

The printer interface is a critical part of PC printer selection and configuration. Generally, you purchase a printer for the port that is available. Most new computers have a USB interface as well as serial and parallel interfaces available, although older computers do not support USB interfaces.

 For more information, see Chapter 4 of David Groth's *A+ Complete Study Guide* (Sybex, 2003).

Lab 4.1: Printers and Printer Interfaces

In this lab, we will discuss different types of printers, their interfaces, and their drivers. The process of installing a printer demonstrates the relationship among these three components. Let's start by looking at the different types of printers.

Types of Printers

Three types of printers are most commonly used today. The following sections give a basic description of each, with some elaboration about the laser printer due to its emphasis on the A+ exam.

EP Laser Printer

The EP (Electrophotographic) laser printer uses static electricity, laser light, and toner to create the image on paper. The parts of an EP printer are illustrated in Figure 4.1.

FIGURE 4.1   The inner workings of an EP printer

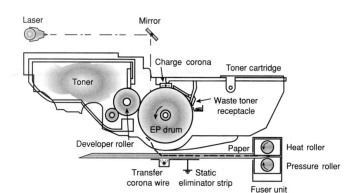

The steps of the printing process are as follows:

Step 1: Cleaning   A rubber blade inside the EP cartridge scrapes off any toner left on the print drum by the last print operation, and a fluorescent lamp discharges the charge on the photo-sensitive drum.

Step 2: Conditioning   A high-voltage corona wire inside the EP cartridge charges the print drum to –600 volts.

Step 3: Writing   A laser scans the drum and flashes on and off in accordance with the data to be printed. Points on the drum that are exposed to the laser light become less negative as the writing continues. These less-negative areas make up the document image on the drum.

Step 4: Developing   The toner receives a negative charge from the developing roller, which is inside the EP cartridge. The negatively charged toner is attracted to the drum and sticks to the areas that were exposed to the laser writing.

Step 5: Transferring   A corona wire charges a sheet of paper positively. As the sheet of paper comes near the drum, the toner on the drum is attracted to the paper. In this way, the image is transferred from the drum to the paper.

Step 6: Fusing   As the paper with the image passes between the heat roller and pressure roller, the polyester resin in the toner melts and is permanently attached to the paper.

LED Laser Printer

An LED laser printer is much like an EP laser printer. However, the writing process uses a bank of LEDs (light-emitting diodes) to create the document image on the drum, and the toner may be replaced by other components.

Dot-Matrix Printer

The main advantage of the dot-matrix printer is its ability to print on multipart forms. You can use multipart forms because the dot-matrix printer is a contact printer. The printhead contains rows of pins that are triggered to form characters as the printhead moves across the paper. (See Figure 4.2.) The printhead pins strike a ribbon much like a typewriter ribbon to transfer the ribbon ink onto the paper.

FIGURE 4.2 Formation of images in a dot-matrix printer

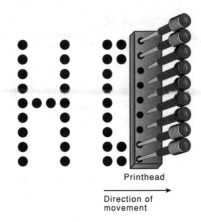

Printhead

Direction of movement

Bubble-Jet Printers

Bubble-jet printers work similarly to dot-matrix printers. A bubble-jet printer uses a print cartridge that contains ink. Instead of striking a ribbon to transfer the image, the bubble jet sprays small droplets of ink onto the paper to form the print characters. The printhead is a mechanism that uses ink-jet nozzles to form the tiny droplets. Because the printhead sprays the ink rather than striking the paper, the printer is much quieter.

A bubble-jet printer may or may not have color capability, and the price of the printer is low compared to other printers. The cost per printed page is fairly high because the print cartridges are expensive and do not print many pages. Some bubble-jet printers print photo-quality prints on photo paper with the use of photo print cartridges. (See Figure 4.3.)

FIGURE 4.3 A typical ink cartridge (size: approximately 3 inches by 1½ inches)

Printer Interfaces and Drivers

The printer interface consists of the hardware and software (drivers) that support the printer. Printer drivers must be selected for the type, brand, and model of printer in use; the operating system installed; and the computer port to which the printer is attached. The printer driver controls the print process. Printer drivers are usually supplied when you purchase a printer; they can often be found on the installation CD for the operating system or can be downloaded from the manufacturer's website. Printers usually work best with the manufacturer's driver specified for the printer and the specific operating system.

Traditionally, the printer was attached to the parallel port (printer port) of a computer, although other ports are being used more and more. The parallel port transfers data one byte at a time and is faster than the serial port, but it requires CPU time for the print process and prevents the processing of other data for a period of time after a print process begins. You configure parallel ports in Device Manager and in CMOS. There are three types of parallel (IEEE1284) ports:

- SPP (standard parallel port) is a unidirectional or simplex port.

- EPP (enhanced parallel port) is a double simplex port. That is, an EPP can transport in either direction but only one direction at a time.

- ECP (enhanced capabilities port) is a new, full-duplex parallel port. *Full duplex* means two-way simultaneous communications. The common telephone is full duplex; both users can talk at the same time.

The main advantage of serial printing is the length of the print cable. A serial cable is typically 25 feet long instead of 10 feet like a parallel cable. The serial port has the advantage of not using CPU time. This feature is used by manufactures of devices like fire alarms—the device can print results without interrupting of monitoring activity. Serial ports transfer data one bit at a time, so they are slower than parallel ports. Few printers have the serial port (RS-232) interface.

The USB (universal serial bus) interface is now the workhorse of the industry and provides an interface for virtually all peripherals. USB ports have high transfer rates and automatically recognize new printers.

Some printers are connected directly to a network. These printers have network interface cards and do not require a computer to act as a print server.

PDAs and laptops often use infrared interfaces. These interfaces permit wireless printing as well as other functions.

Upon completion of this lab, you will be able to:

- Identify printer interfaces
- Configure the parallel printer port

Set Up

For this exercise, you will need a PC with Windows installed. You may want to complete this lab in windows 98, Windows 2000, and Windows XP. You will want to see the differences in how to get to the settings in the different operating systems.

Exercise

In this exercise, you will record CMOS port settings and Device Manager parallel port settings.

1. Boot to the CMOS and locate the settings for the serial (COM) and parallel ports. Do not make any changes to CMOS settings.

2. Record the settings for COM 1 and COM 2, if available, and the parallel port:

   Serial port address and IRQ settings:

   _____

   Parallel port address and IRQ settings:

   _____

   Parallel port mode: SPP (Normal) EPP ECP

3. Use the appropriate sequence to open Device Manager:

   In Windows 98:

   > Start ➤ Settings ➤ Control Panel ➤ System ➤ Device Manager

   In Windows 2000:

   > Right-click My Computer ➤ Manage ➤ Device Manager

   In Windows XP:

   > Start ➤ Control Panel ➤ Administrative Tools ➤ Computer Management ➤ Device Manager

4. In Device Manager, click the plus sign next to Ports.

5. Right-click the LPT port and then click Properties. Click on the Resources tab. Record the IRQ and I/O address for this port.

   IRQ:

   _____

   I/O Address:

   _____

Lab Report 4.1

1. What is the sequence for opening Device Manager?
    In Windows 98:

    _____

    In Windows 2000:

    _____

    In Windows XP:

    _____

2. What type of system is most likely to use the infrared interface for the printer port?

    _____

3. List the three types of parallel ports, with the most advanced type of port listed first.

    _____

    _____

    _____

Lab 4.2: Installing an Imaginary Printer in a Windows 98 System

Printer installation requires the installation of a printer driver from the operating system installation CD, the printer manufacturer, or the Internet. Printers have traditionally been attached to the parallel port, but they often connect to the USB port or to a serial port (COM 1 or COM 2).

Upon completion of this lab, you will be able to:

- Install a printer in a Windows 98 system
- Investigate printer properties

Set Up

For this exercise, you will need a working Windows 98 computer.

Exercise

In this exercise, you will complete the printer installation without having a printer attached to your computer. If you have a printer attached, you can install an additional printer by following this procedure; you will also be able to test the installation by printing a test page.

Installing an imaginary printer is often a good idea while you're learning. Doing so gives you a printer to experiment with without the possibility of misconfiguring your real printer.

1. Boot to the Desktop and use the following sequence to see which printers are installed in your system:

   Start ➢ Settings ➢ Printers

   Record any printers that appear in the Printers folder:

   _____

2. Double-click the Add Printer icon and then click Next to begin the installation.

3. Select Local Printer and click Next.

4. In the first Add Printer Wizard screen, select a manufacturer and printer model. The choices do not matter, because you are installing an imaginary printer. (See Figure 4.4.)

FIGURE 4.4   Selecting the printer driver to install

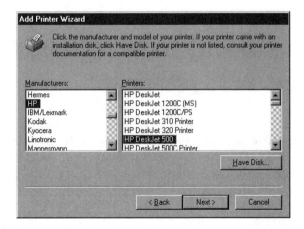

5. Select a printer port and click Next.

6. Enter a printer name and click Next.

7. *Do not* print a test page—there is no printer.

8. If requested, insert the Windows 98 installation CD, select the file source, and click OK. The source is the CD-ROM drive and Win 98 (D:\WIN98).

9. The printer icon should appear in the Printers folder. Right-click the printer icon and then list the options available. The options may be different for different printers:

_____

_____

_____

10. Select Properties. Record the printer port from the General tab and the printer driver from the Driver tab:

_____

_____

Lab Report 4.2

1. If the Printers folder is open, how can you determine which port the printer is using?

_____

_____

2. How do you start the printer installation process?

_____

_____

3. If you are installing the printer driver from the operating system installation CD, how is the driver source identified in the Add Printer Wizard?

    _____

    _____

4. If you do not have a printer driver for your printer, where can you usually get a driver?

    _____

    _____

Lab 4.3: Installing an Imaginary Printer in a Windows XP System

The process involved in installing an imaginary printer in XP varies slightly from the previous lab. Upon completion of this lab, you will be able to:

- Install a printer in a Windows XP system.
- Investigate printer properties.

Set Up

For this exercise, you will need a working Windows XP computer.

Exercise

In this exercise, you will complete the printer installation without having a printer attached to your computer. If you have a printer attached, the procedure is the same, except that you can test the installation by printing a test page.

1. Boot to the Desktop and use the following sequence to see which printers are installed in your system:

    Start ➤ Control Panel ➤ Printers and Other Hardware ➤ Printers and Faxes

    Record any printers that appear in the Printers and Faxes folder:

    _____

2. In the Printers and Faxes window, select Add Printer to begin the installation.

3. Click Next in the Add Printer Wizard.

4. Select the Local Printer Attached to This Computer option and click Next.

5. Select the Use the Following Port – (LPT1) option and click Next.

6. Select a manufacturer and printer. The choices do not matter, because you are not completing the installation.

7. Type in a printer name. Answer No to the question *Do you want to use this printer as the default printer?* and click Next.

8. Do not share the printer. Click Next.

9. *Do not* print a test page—there is no printer.

10. If requested, insert the Windows XP installation CD, select the file source, and then click OK. The source is the CD-ROM drive and Win XP (D:\I386).

11. Record the printer settings displayed in the Completing the Add Printer Wizard window:

_____

_____

_____

Click Finish.

12. In the Printer and Faxes window, right-click the printer icon and select Properties.

13. In the printer properties display, select Ports and record the port used by the printer:

_____

14. Return to the Desktop.

Lab Report 4.3

1. If the Printers and Faxes folder is open, how can you determine which port the printer is using?

_____

_____

2. How do you start the printer installation process?

   _____

   _____

   _____

3. If you are installing the printer driver from the operating system installation CD, how is the driver source identified in the Add Printer Wizard?

   _____

   _____

4. If you do not have a printer driver for your printer, where can you usually get a driver?

   _____

   _____

Answers to Lab Reports

Lab Report 4.1

1. Here are the steps for each version:

    Windows 98:

    > Start ➢ Settings ➢ Control Panel ➢ System ➢ Device Manager

    Windows 2000:

    > Right-click My Computer ➢ Manage ➢ Device Manager

    Windows XP:

    > Start ➢ Control Panel ➢ Administrative Tools ➢ Computer Management ➢ Device Manager

2. The infrared interface is used by PDAs and laptops.

3. In order of sophistication: ECP, EPP, and SPP.

Lab Report 4.2

1. Right-click the printer icon and select Properties. The port is found on the General tab.

2. Open the printer folder with the following sequence: Start ➢ Settings ➢ Printers. Then, double-click the Add Printer icon.

3. D:\WIN98, if the CD-ROM drive is drive D:.

4. The driver can usually be downloaded from the Internet.

Lab Report 4.3

1. Right-click the printer icon, select Properties, and then select Ports.

2. Open the Printers and Faxes folder with the following sequence: Start ➢ Control Panel ➢ Printers and Other Hardware ➢ Printers and Faxes. Then select the Add Printer icon.

3. D:\I386, if the CD-ROM drive is drive D:.

4. The driver can usually be downloaded from the Internet.

Chapter

5

Basic Networking

LABS YOU WILL PERFORM IN THIS CHAPTER:

- ✓ Lab 5.1: Identifying Network Topologies, Cables, and Connectors
- ✓ Lab 5.2: Understanding Network Configurations

A network connects two or more computers together to share information or resources. A LAN (local area network) connects computers in the same office, whereas a WAN (wide area network) connects computers that are great distances apart. A LAN may be connected to a WAN such as the Internet. In peer-to-peer networks, all computers act as both servers and workstations; server-based networks have one computer that provides centralized control. Server-based networks offer more security but require a network manager.

In this chapter we will explore PC networks by examining existing network topologies and their cables, and identifying network configurations and settings.

 For more information, see Chapter 5 of David Groth's *A+ Complete Study Guide* (Sybex, 2003).

Lab 5.1: Identifying Network Topologies, Cables, and Connectors

Upon completion of this lab, you will be able to:

- Determine the local topology of your network
- Identify network cables and connectors

Before we begin, you need to know a few networking basics.

Topologies

A *topology* describes the general layout of the network connections. LANs use several types of physical topologies (cable connection variations) and logical topologies (how the network messages travel). You should be able to identify the following networking configurations:

Bus Topology   The bus topology has a single cable that runs to every computer in the network. Hubs or switches are not needed; however, repeaters are used to extend network length.

Star Topology   The star topology uses a hub or switch as a central connection device. Every computer in the network is connected to the central connection device. The star is cheap, easy to install, easy to reconfigure, and fault tolerant. Hubs and switches can be connected together to extend the network.

Ring Topology   In a physical ring topology, each computer is connected to two other computers to form a circle. The physical ring is difficult to reconfigure, and the entire network goes down if any computer is removed from the ring.

Logical rings connect the computers to a central connection device called a multistation access unit (MAU or MSAU). The MAU creates the ring in its circuitry, thereby making the ring easier to configure and manage. MAUs can be connected using the Ring In and Ring Out ports to extend the network.

Mesh Topology   In the mesh topology, each device is connected to every other device with a direct cable connection. The mesh is very difficult to construct and reconfigure. However, it is very fault tolerant.

Hybrid Topology   A hybrid topology is a mixture of networks, each using its own topology. The hybrid topology uses the best features of each topology.

Media Access Methods

A *media access method* is the way the computer accesses the physical medium. It lays out the rules of when and how a computer can put packets onto the network. You should be able to identify the various media used to connect a network:

Ethernet   Ethernet uses an access protocol called Carrier Sense Multiple Access with Collision Detection (CSMA/CD). *Carrier Sense* means that the computer listens to see if anyone else is already talking when it wants to put a packet on the wire. *Multiple Access* allows all the computers to listen at the same time; and, all the computers have equal access to the media. Because all computers have equal access, two computers will frequently attempt to put packets on the media at the same time. When this happens, a collision occurs. Both computers listen to detect if a collision has occurred. If it has, both computers stop transmitting and time themselves out for a random period before they listen again to see if they are clear to transmit. The Ethernet media is the wire that carries the signal between computers. It is often called the wire even though some media is wireless.

Token Ring   Token Ring uses a token on the network to control when and how computers are allowed to put a packet on the wire. A free token is passed on the network from one computer to the next in line. When a computer receives the free token, it either passes it to the next computer, if it has nothing to transmit, or it captures the token and then loads a packet into the token. As the loaded token is passed from computer to computer, each one looks at the token's header to see if the token is for that computer. If the computer is not the destination computer, the token is retransmitted to the next computer in line. When the destination is reached, the destination computer places an acknowledgement on the token and sends it back to the source computer. When the source computer gets the acknowledgement back, the token is released by simply flipping the two bits on the token.

Thicknet 10Base5   Thicknet gets its name from the size of the wire that is used. It is a coaxial cable with a center core wire that is insulated and shielded to reduce the amount of electromagnetic interference (EMI). Its cable can extend 500 meters without needing a repeater. It is used primarily to create a bus topology frequently called a *backbone*, because of the distance the signal can travel and its immunity to interference. Thicknet is very rigid, which makes it difficult to work with. Computers connect to the cable using a vampire tap that pierces the insulation and shielding. The network adapter has an AUI connector.

Thinnet 10Base2   Thinnet also gets its name from the size of the wire used. It is a coaxial cable but thinner than the cable used in Thicknet. Its cable can carry a signal 185 meters. Computers use a BNC T-connector to attach themselves to the network. The network adapter also uses a BNC connector.

Twisted Pair 10/100BaseT   The most popular type of cable in use today is twisted pair. It comes in two basic varieties: shielded and unshielded. Shielded twisted pair (STP) uses a wire mesh shield to help protect the wire from EMI. Unshielded twisted pair (UTP) uses the twists in the pairs to reduce the amount of cross talk. The network adapter uses an RJ-45 connector.

Fiber Optic 100BaseFL   Fiber optic has two main advantages over copper cable. First, fiber can extend greater distances—up to 2,000 meters. Second, it is immune to EMI because it uses light pulses instead of electrical signals.

Set Up

For this exercise, you will need a network-ready computer.

Exercise

In this lab, you will explore the different types of topologies, cables, and connectors.

1.   Draw an example of a bus topology.

2. Draw an example of a ring topology.

3. Draw an example of a star topology.

4. Examine the back of your computer and determine the type of network cable used. You will probably find an RJ-45 connector on Category 5, twisted pair cable. The RJ-45 connector looks much like a telephone connector, but it is larger. You may find a coaxial cable that looks like a cable television cable. The coaxial cable is commonly used in a 10Base2 (Thinnet) network. Record the type of cable found:

_____

5. Trace the network wiring and try to determine the physical topology of your network. Record the topology.

_____

Lab Report 5.1

1. Identify the following physical topologies:

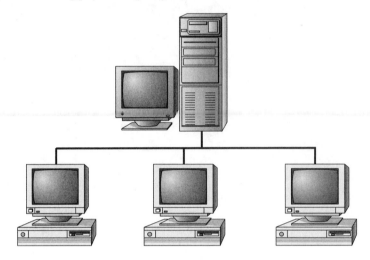

A. _____

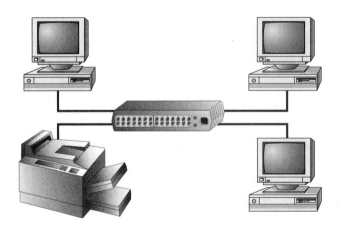

B. _____

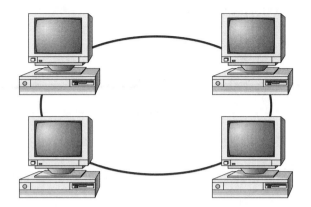

C. _____

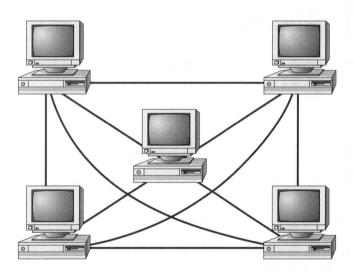

D. _____

2. What is one advantage of Thicknet over Thinnet?

_____

3. What type of network cable has a connector similar to a phone jack?

_____

4. List the five common topologies used by LANs.

_____

_____

_____

_____

_____

Lab 5.2: Understanding Network Configurations

Upon completion of this lab, you will be able to:

- Examine your network configuration

Set Up

For this exercise, you will need a Windows PC that is installed in a network.

Exercise

In this lab, you will examine your network and record its features.

Examining Your Windows 98 Workstation

To examine your Windows 98 workstation,

1. Boot to the Desktop and use the following to open the network configuration tab:

   Start ➤ Settings ➤ Control Panel ➤ Network ➤ Configuration Tab

Record the Network Card installed:

_____

(The name of the network card is displayed by itself after the protocols that are being used.)

2. Select File and Print Sharing and record the resources being shared:

    _____

3. Select the Identification tab and record your computer name:

    _____

    Also record the workgroup name:

    _____

4. Select the Access Control tab and record the access control enabled:

    _____

5. Return to the Desktop and open My Computer. Observe the Drive C: icon in the My Computer window. If the drive C: icon has a hand under it, the drive is shared on the network. Is your drive C: shared? Y N

6. Use the following to display your TCP/IP configuration information:

    Start ➢ Programs ➢ MS-DOS Prompt

7. When the DOS Prompt opens, type `winipcfg`.

8. Note the IP address configuration (you might have to scroll through the protocols to accurately see LAN configuration parameters):

    IP address:

    _____

    Subnet mask:

    _____

    Default gateway:

    _____

    DNS:

    _____

Examining Your Windows 2000 Workstation

To examine your Windows 2000 workstation,

1. Boot to the Desktop and use the following to open the network connections:

   Start ➤ Settings ➤ Network and Dialup Connections

2. In the Network and Dialup Connections screen, right-click Local Area Connection and choose Properties.

   Record the network card installed:

   _____

3. To observe document sharing, open My Documents and highlight a folder with a hand under it. The hand indicates a shared folder. Right-click Folder ➤ Sharing and then click Permissions.

   Is full control given? Y N

4. To see all the shares on your computer, right-click My Computer and use the following:

   Manage ➤ System Tools ➤ Shared Folders ➤ Shares

   Record the shares:

   _____

5. Use the following to display your computer and workgroup name:

   Start ➤ Settings ➤ Control Panel ➤ System ➤ Network Identification

   Record the computer name and workgroup name:

   _____

   _____

6. Use the following to display your TCP/IP configuration information:

   Start ➤ Programs ➤ MS-DOS Prompt

7. When the DOS Prompt opens, type **ipconfig /all**.

8. Note the IP address configuration:

   IP address:

   _____

Subnet mask:

_____

Default gateway:

_____

DNS:

_____

Examining Your Windows XP Workstation

To examine your Windows XP workstation,

1. Boot to the Desktop and use the following to open the network connections:

    Start ➤ Control Panel ➤ Network and Internet Connections ➤ Network Connections

2. In the Network Connections screen, right-click Local Area Connection, choose Properties, and click the General tab.

    Record the network card installed:

    _____

3. Use the following to access the document sharing:

    Start ➤ My Documents ➤ Share This Folder

    Is the Share This Folder on the Network option checked? Y N

4. Use the following to display your computer and workgroup name:

    Start ➤ Control Panel ➤ Performance and Maintenance ➤ System ➤ Computer Name tab

    Record the computer name:

    _____

5. Return to the Desktop and open My Computer. Observe the Drive C: icon in the My Computer window. If the drive C: icon has a hand under it, the drive is shared on the network. Is your drive C: shared? Y N

6. Use the following to display your TCP/IP configuration information:

    Start ➤ Programs ➤ MS-DOS Prompt

7. When the DOS Prompt opens, type **ipconfig /all**.

8. Note the IP address configuration:

    IP address:

    _____

    Subnet mask:

    _____

    Default gateway:

    _____

    DNS:

    _____

Lab Report 5.2

1. How did your computer's IP address get configured?

    _____

    _____

2. What utility shows your computer's IP address in Windows 98? In Windows 2000? In Windows XP?

    _____

    _____

    _____

3. What shares exist on your computer?

_____

_____

4. What utility shows the shares on your computer?

_____

Answers to Lab Report 5.1

1.
   - **A.** Bus
   - **B.** Star
   - **C.** Ring
   - **D.** Mesh
2. Thicknet offers a longer distance for the network.
3. The RJ-45, Category 5, twisted pair connector looks like a large phone jack.
4. Bus, star, ring, mesh, and hybrid

Answers to Lab Report 5.2

1. It depends on the computer. Most computers are configured to use automatic configuration or DHCP.
2. In Windows 98, you use the `WINIPCFG` utility. In Windows 2000 and Windows XP, you use the `IPCONFIG` utility.
3. It depends on your computer. At minimum, you should see C$, D$, and IPC$.
4. The Computer Management utility shows the shares in the Windows 2000/XP operating systems.

Chapter

6

Building a PC

LABS YOU WILL PERFORM IN THIS CHAPTER:

- ✓ Lab 6.1: Removing and Replacing a Motherboard
- ✓ Lab 6.2: Removing and Inserting Memory
- ✓ Lab 6.3: Removing and Replacing a Power Supply
- ✓ Lab 6.4: Installing a CD-ROM, CD-R, CD-RW, or DVD Drive
- ✓ Lab 6.5: Collecting Resource Information
- ✓ Lab 6.6: CMOS Setup

As an A+ certified technician, you may find yourself needing to replace various FRUs (Field Replaceable Units) in the course of your work. In this chapter, we will go over the basic instructions for removing and replacing key computer components.

For more information, see Chapter 6 of David Groth's *A+ Complete Study Guide* (Sybex, 2003).

Lab 6.1: Removing and Replacing a Motherboard

The most difficult part of motherboard removal and replacement is keeping track of what goes where. Do not rely on your memory. Take notes, draw diagrams, and mark wires as you remove components. Without this information, reassembly becomes a guessing game. Confirm that your computer is operational before you open the computer case and after you complete the lab.

Upon completion of this lab, you will be able to:

- Remove and replace expansion cards
- Identify major components and document the connections to the motherboard and expansion boards
- Remove and reinstall a motherboard

Set Up

For this exercise, you will need an operational PC.

Exercise

In this lab, you will verify that your computer is operational, remove the motherboard, reinstall the motherboard, and ensure that the computer is again operational.

Testing the Computer for Proper Operation

To test the computer for proper operation,

1. Boot the computer.
2. Access all drives to verify that the computer is operational.
3. Record the CMOS hard drive information.

Removing the Motherboard

To remove the motherboard,

1. Shut down the computer.

2. Turn off the power to all peripherals that are attached to the computer.

3. Sketch the back of the computer as you disconnect all external cables.

4. Remove the computer cover.

As soon as the computer cover is removed, ESD (electrostatic discharge) becomes a hazard to the computer.

5. Wear an antistatic wrist strap and attach it to the computer case. If no antistatic wrist strap is available, equalize the static charge by frequently touching a bare portion of the computer case.

6. Draw a rough sketch of the motherboard and show the location and use of each expansion slot. Sometimes an expansion card will not work if it is moved to a different slot.

7. Draw a sketch of any expansion card that has wires or cables connected to it.

8. Carefully add to your sketches the connection blocks and cables that attach to the expansion cards. Ribbon cables have a stripe on one edge to identify pin 1. Without this information, you may not be able to identify the connection when you reinstall the motherboard.

9. As you remove the expansion cards from the computer, disconnect all cables from them. Place the expansion cards on an antistatic mat.

10. The motherboard should now be exposed. Carefully draw the motherboard connection blocks for all cables that attach to the motherboard. For ribbon cables, note pin 1. For all other wires, be sure to show the color and function of each wire. If no distinguishing marks are available, you can use a permanent marker to make notes on the cable.

11. Remove any screws that connect the motherboard to the case.

12. Remove the motherboard from the case. The plastic or brass standoffs may permit you to move the motherboard to the side and lift it out. You may have to compress the standoffs with long-nose pliers while gently lifting the system board. Use extreme care with the motherboard because bending or dropping it can easily damage it.

Installing a Motherboard

To install a motherboard,

1. If the memory is not already installed, install it.

2. Install plastic or brass standoffs if they are needed.

3. Align the keyboard connector and the expansion slots with the holes in the case.

4. Secure the motherboard with the screws you removed.

5. Install the expansion cards. Use your drawings and notes to ensure that all cables and cards are installed in their original locations and are connected properly.

6. Attach the cables and internal components. ATX power supply connectors connect only one way; however, if AT power supply cables are incorrectly connected to the motherboard, the motherboard may be damaged. The black wires on the P8 and P9 connectors are installed *black to black*.

7. Reassemble the computer.

8. Boot the computer and access all the drives to verify that the computer is operational.

Lab Report 6.1

1. During reassembly, why do you need to place expansion cards in their original slots?

   _____

   _____

2. What type of motherboard can be damaged if you reverse the power connectors?

   _____

   _____

3. Why should you sketch the cable and wire connections between the motherboard and the case?

   _____

   _____

4. What is the function of the stripe on ribbon cables?

_____

_____

Lab 6.2: Removing and Inserting Memory

The main memory (RAM) on motherboards is usually divided into several banks. The banks are numbered, and the lowest numbered bank is zero (0). Usually, if the lowest-numbered bank is not filled, the computer does not use the memory.

Because each computer has several possible memory insertion configurations, consult the motherboard specifications for memory configurations. In order to function properly, each memory bank must be populated with memory of the same type and speed. Static electricity can damage the memory modules, so it is important that you wear an antistatic wrist strap and use antistatic mats.

Upon completion of this lab, you will be able to:

-   Determine the amount of memory
-   Remove memory modules
-   Install memory modules

Set Up

For this exercise, you will need an operational PC.

Exercise

In this lab, you will determine the amount of memory installed in a computer, remove a bank of memory, determine the amount of memory remaining, and reinstall the bank of memory. There are several ways to view the total RAM installed, but the MEM command works in all versions of Windows.

Determining the Total RAM Present

To determine the total RAM present,

1. Boot the computer and start a Windows DOS session or boot to DOS.

    For a Windows 9x computer, use the following sequence to obtain a DOS prompt:

    Start ➤ Programs ➤ MS-DOS Prompt

For a Windows NT computer, use the following sequence to obtain a command prompt:

Start ➤ Programs ➤ Command Prompt

For a Windows 2000 computer, use the following sequence to obtain a command prompt:

Start ➤ Programs ➤ Accessories ➤ Command Prompt

For a Windows XP computer, use the following sequence to obtain a command prompt:

Start ➤ All Programs ➤ Accessories ➤ Command Prompt

2. To determine the total memory installed in your computer, enter the following at the C: prompt:

`C:\>MEM`

Record the total RAM installed:

_____

(Because some RAM is utilized for expanded memory and other issues, the reported total RAM may be about 300KB less than the memory module size.)

Removing Memory Modules

To remove memory modules,

1. Shut down the power and unplug all cables from the computer.

WARNING   Memory modules are very susceptible to ESD (electrostatic discharge). Use ESD precautions, and place the memory modules on an antistatic mat when they are not installed in a computer.

2. Open the case and locate the memory.

3. Remove the memory modules from the highest-numbered populated bank.

For SIMMs, release the memory module clips by pressing the clips outward with your thumbs. When the memory module is free, lift it from the socket.

For DIMMs, press down on the module jacks and then lift the memory module. Repeat these steps until the bank is empty.

4. Replace the cover, reconnect all cables, and boot the computer. If all the RAM has been removed, the computer will not boot. If the PC does boot, it should have less available RAM due to the removal of RAM from the higher numbered bank.

5. Use MEM to determine the quantity of memory installed:

`C:\>MEM`

The memory should now be less than reported in step 2 of the previous section.

Installing Memory Modules

To install memory modules,

1. Shut down the power and unplug all cables from the computer.

 WARNING Memory modules are very susceptible to ESD. Use ESD precautions, and place the memory modules on an antistatic mat when they are not installed in a computer.

2. Open the case and locate the memory sockets.
3. Install the memory modules in the lowest-numbered, unpopulated memory bank.

    For SIMMs, hold the module at a slight angle and align the notch and pin 1. Gently press down on the module and push it into the lock position.

    For DIMMs, align the module slots with the socket keys and then press the module into the memory slot.

4. Install the rest of the modules in the bank.
5. Replace the cover, reconnect all cables, and boot the computer.
6. Determine the quantity of memory installed:

    `C:\>MEM`

    The total RAM reported should show an increase.

Lab Report 6.2

1. How can you reduce the static electricity hazard for RAM?

    _____

    _____

2. What is one method you can use to determine the amount of memory installed in a computer?

    _____

    _____

    _____

3. If you have enough memory to fill only one memory bank, which bank should you fill?

_____

_____

_____

4. What does RAM do in a computer system?

_____

_____

_____

_____

Lab 6.3: Removing and Replacing a Power Supply

Power supplies are not usually considered to be repairable, but frequently they need to be replaced. Sometimes, defective power supplies cause intermittent troubles that are difficult to pinpoint.

Power supplies come in many styles and in many power ratings. The power supply you use as a replacement must be the same style as the power supply being replaced, or it will not physically fit the computer case. The power supply you use as a replacement must also have a wattage rating that's the same as or higher than that of the power supply being replaced.

Upon completion of this lab, you will be able to:

- Remove a power supply from a computer

- Install a power supply in a computer

Set Up

For this exercise, you will need an operational PC.

Exercise

In this lab, you will remove the power supply and replace a power supply.

Removing a Computer Power Supply

To remove a computer power supply,

1. Record the CMOS hard-drive information:

   Heads:

   _____

   Cylinders:

   _____

   Sectors:

   _____

2. Sketch the back of the computer and show where each cable is attached. Then, disconnect all the external cables from the computer.

AT computers have 120 volts applied to the panel-mounted power switch any time the power cable is attached to the computer. The voltage is a safety hazard to the technician. If you come in contact with the 120 volts, serious injury or death could occur.

ATX computers have 5 volts on the motherboard any time the computer is attached to the power cable. The voltage is a safety hazard to the motherboard when the case is open. If a screw or some other object drops into the computer and short-circuits the motherboard, the motherboard will be destroyed.

3. Remove the computer cover to expose the power supply. As soon as the cover is removed, ESD (electrostatic discharge) precautions must be used.

4. Disconnect the power connector from the motherboard.

   AT computers have two power connectors (P8 and P9) on the motherboard.

   ATX computers have one power connector on the motherboard.

5. Disconnect the other power-supply cable leads from the drives, fans, and so on. Each piece of hardware that you disconnect must be reconnected to the replacement power supply. You should make a list of the hardware items as you disconnect them so you can use the list as a guide when you reassemble the computer.

6. The power switch is located on the front panel of most computers. Generally, you should remove the switch from the case and leave it connected to the power supply.

7. Remove the power-supply mounting screws and then lift the power supply out of the case.

Do not plug the power supply into a wall outlet unless it is connected to a motherboard! Doing so could produce high voltage and cause the power supply to self-destruct.

Installing a Power Supply

To install a power supply,

1. Wear an antistatic wrist strap to protect the computer from ESD, and make sure no external cables are connected to the computer or the power supply.

2. Place the power supply in the computer case's power-supply support bracket, and then install the mounting screws.

3. For an ATX computer, the power switch connects to the motherboard.

   For an AT computer, route the power-switch cable in a safe location, and attach the power switch to the case.

4. Attach the power supply to the motherboard.

5. If you have an AT computer, attach connectors P8 and P9 to the motherboard with the black wires next to each other.

6. On an ATX computer, the motherboard power connector is keyed and will fit only one way.

The P8 and P9 connectors are connected with the black wires next to each other (black to black). If the P8 and P9 connectors are reversed, the motherboard will probably be destroyed.

7. Connect the other power supply output leads to the drives, fans, and so on.

8. Remove your antistatic wrist strap, install the computer case, and connect the external cables to the computer.

9. Boot the computer.

Lab Report 6.3

1. When is voltage available to the front-mounted power switch in an AT computer? How many volts are available?

_____

_____

_____

_____

2. When is voltage available in an ATX computer motherboard? How many volts are available?

_____

_____

_____

_____

3. When referring to P8 and P9 connectors, what does the term *black to black* mean?

_____

_____

_____

_____

4. If the P8 and P9 connectors were reversed, what would probably happen?

_____

_____

_____

_____

_____

Lab 6.4: Installing a CD-ROM, CD-R, CD-RW, or DVD Drive

Most new software comes on CD-ROM discs. So, a computer without a CD-ROM drive cannot use the new software that is available. For best performance, the CD-ROM drive should be connected as the master drive on the secondary IDE interface controller, and the boot drive (drive C:) should be connected as the master drive on the primary IDE interface controller.

Upon completion of this lab, you will be able to:

- Install a CD-ROM, CD-R, CD-RW, or DVD drive in a Windows system

- Install the software required to support the CD-ROM drive

Set Up

For this exercise, you will need:

- A working Windows 9x computer with an IDE interface hard drive

- An IDE interface CD-ROM, CD-R, CD-RW, or DVD drive

- Mounting hardware for the CD-ROM drive

- A Windows 98 startup disk

- A CD-ROM driver disk

Exercise

In this lab, you will install an IDE (ATAPI) interface CD-ROM drive. Sometimes, the sound card CD-ROM controller is used; however, in this lab, you will connect to the primary IDE interface or to the secondary IDE interface.

Installing a Windows CD-ROM Drive in a One-Port System

To install a Windows CD-ROM drive in a one-port system,

1. Set the hard-drive jumpers to the master position. The jumper positions are usually documented on the drive. If you are not installing a new hard drive or CD-ROM, you will need to remove them first.

2. Set the CD-ROM drive jumpers to the slave position. The jumper positions are usually documented on the drive.

3. Mount the CD-ROM drive in the drive bay.

4. Connect the second port on the hard-drive IDE cable to the CD-ROM drive. Be sure to connect the striped edge of the ribbon cable to pin 1 of the CD-ROM drive.

5. Connect the power cable to the CD-ROM drive.

6. Boot the computer to the Desktop and look for the CD-ROM drive in My Computer.

7. If the CD-ROM icon does not appear in My Computer, use the following sequence to install the CD-ROM drive:

      Control Panel ➤ Add New Hardware

   If the CD-ROM icon still does not appear in My Computer, go back to step 1.

8. For Windows versions other than Windows XP, you will probably be asked to insert a device driver disk to enable features other than reading a CD.

Installing a Windows CD-ROM Drive in a Two-Port System

To install a Windows CD-ROM drive in a two-port system,

1. Obtain an IDE ribbon cable and connect it to the second IDE port. Do not disturb the first IDE port or the hard drive(s) attached to it. Be sure to connect the striped edge of the ribbon cable to pin 1 of the IDE port.

2. Set the CD-ROM drive jumpers to the master position.

3. Mount the CD-ROM drive in the drive bay.

4. Connect the second IDE port cable to the CD-ROM drive. Be sure to connect the striped edge of the ribbon cable to pin 1 of the CD-ROM drive.

5. Connect the power cable to the CD-ROM drive.

6. Boot the computer and look for the CD-ROM drive in My Computer.

7. If the CD-ROM icon does not appear in My Computer, use the following sequence to install the CD-ROM drive:

      Control Panel ➤ Add New Hardware

   If the CD-ROM icon still does not appear in My Computer, go back to Step 1.

8. For Windows versions other than Windows XP, you will probably be asked to insert the device driver disk to enable features other than reading a CD.

Lab Report 6.4

1. In what circumstance would you set the CD-ROM drives to the slave position during the installation of a CD-ROM drive?

   _____

   _____

   _____

   _____

2. How is the master or slave selection set on a typical CD-ROM drive?

   _____

   _____

   _____

   _____

3. For the best performance, the bootable hard drive should be installed as the master drive on the primary IDE interface. Where should the CD-ROM be attached for best performance?

   _____

   _____

   _____

   _____

4. How can you recognize the pin-1 edge of the IDE data cable?

_____

_____

_____

_____

_____

Lab 6.5: Collecting Resource Information

When you are adding a new element to a computer, you need to ensure that it does not compete with other components for resources. In this lab, you'll properly determine IRQ assignments and I/O addresses. There are a couple of concepts you should be familiar with:

Interrupts   The interrupt request (IRQ) is a bus feature that permits a device to signal the processor to get the processor's immediate attention. An interrupt indicates that an event requiring the processor's attention has occurred, causing the processor to suspend and save its current activity and then branch to an interrupt service routine. This service routine processes the interrupt (whether it was generated by a keystroke or a mouse click) and, when it's complete, returns control to the suspended process. Ideally, each device has its own IRQ number.

I/O Addresses   The processor treats each device as a memory location and sends information to that address or reads information from that address. This I/O address is unique for each device that communicates with the processor.

Upon completion of this lab, you will be able to:

- Determine a computer's IRQ assignments
- Determine a computer's I/O address assignments.

Set Up

For this exercise, you will need an operational computer with DOS, Windows 98, Windows 2000, or Windows XP installed.

Exercise

In this exercise, we'll go over resource information for the versions of Windows in use today.

Collecting DOS Resource Information

To collect DOS resource information,

1. Boot to the C: drive.

2. At the DOS prompt, enter **VER** to display the DOS version installed:

   C:\>**VER**

   Record the DOS version:

   _____

3. Change to the DOS directory and enter **MSD** to run the Microsoft Diagnostic utility:

   C:\>**CD DOS**
   C:\DOS>**MSD**

4. To access the IRQ status, press the letter U on the keyboard (the colored letter) in the MSD screen.

5. Record the displayed system information in Table 6.1.

TABLE 6.1   DOS IRQ Information

IRQ #	I/O Address	Hardware Using the Setting:
IRQ 1	_____	_____
IRQ 2	_____	_____
IRQ 3	_____	_____
IRQ 4	_____	_____
IRQ 5	_____	_____
IRQ 7	_____	_____

6. To exit the MSD program:
   A. Press Alt+F to bring down the menu.
   B. Press X to return to the C: prompt.

Determining Windows 98 Resource Information

To determine Windows 98 resource information,

1. To open the System Information window, use the following sequence:

    Start ➤ Programs ➤ Accessories ➤ System Tools ➤ System Information

    Record the processor type, memory size, and OS revision:

    _____

2. In the System Information window, click the plus sign (+) next to Hardware Resources. When the branch expands, click the IRQ branch and record the hardware that uses the IRQs in Table 6.2.

3. Click the I/O branch and record the I/O address for the printer port (LPT1).

4. Click the DMA branch and record the hardware using DMA 2.

5. To view the hard-drive properties, right-click the drive C: icon in the My Computer window and then select Properties. Record the hard drive capacity and the amount of free hard-drive space:

    _____

TABLE 6.2   Windows 98 IRQ information

Resource	Hardware Using the Setting:
Printer Port I/O	_____
IRQ 3	_____
IRQ 4	_____
IRQ 5	_____
IRQ 6	_____
IRQ 7	_____
DMA 2	_____

Determining Windows 2000 Resource Information

To determine Windows 2000 resource information,

1. To obtain the processor type, memory size, and version of Windows that is installed, boot to the Windows Desktop and use the following sequence:

    Start ➤ Programs ➤ Accessories ➤ System Tools ➤ System Information

    Record the processor type, total memory, and OS version (revision) in Table 6.3.

2. To obtain the IRQ assignments in a Windows system, use this alternate sequence from the Windows Desktop:

    Right click My Computer and choose Manage ➤ System Tools ➤ System Information

    In the System Information window, click the plus sign (+) next to Hardware Resources. When the branch expands, click the IRQs branch. Record the IRQ information.

3. To view the hard-drive properties, right-click the drive C: icon in the My Computer window and then select Properties. Record the hard-drive capacity and free space in Table 6.3.

4. To obtain detailed memory information, use Task Manager. Right-click the Taskbar, select Task Manager, and click the Performance tab. Record the Physical Memory total and the Physical Memory Available:

TABLE 6.3   Windows 2000 IRQ Information

System Data	Your System:	IRQ #	Hardware Using the Setting:
Microprocessor	_____	IRQ 1	_____
Memory (Total)	_____	IRQ 3	_____
OS Revision	_____	IRQ 4	_____
Drive C: (Capacity)	_____	IRQ 5	_____
Drive C: Free Hard Drive Space	_____	IRQ 7	_____

Determining Windows 2000 Resource Information

To determine Windows 2000 resource information,

1. To obtain the processor type, memory size, and version of Windows that is installed, boot to the Windows Desktop and use the following sequence:

    Start ➤ All Programs ➤ Accessories ➤ System Tools ➤ System Information

Record the processor type, total memory, and OS version (revision) in Table 6.4.

2. To obtain the IRQ assignments in a Windows XP system, click the plus sign (+) next to Hardware Resources. When the branch expands, click the IRQs branch. Record the IRQ information in Table 6.4.

3. To view the hard-drive properties, right-click the My Computer icon in the Start menu and then select System Information. Click on the Drive tab and select the C: drive from the drop-down menu. Record the hard-drive capacity and free space in Table 6.4.

4. To obtain detailed memory information, click the Memory tab. Record the Physical Memory total and the Physical Memory Available:

TABLE 6.4   Windows XP System Information

System Data	Your System:	IRQ #	Hardware Using the Setting:
Microprocessor	_____	IRQ 1	_____
Memory (Total)	_____	IRQ 3	_____
OS Revision	_____	IRQ 4	_____
Drive C: (Capacity)	_____	IRQ 5	_____
Drive C: Free Hard Drive Space	_____	IRQ 9	_____

Lab Report 6.5

1. Which DOS utility displays system resource information?

_____

_____

_____

_____

2. Where is the most reliable hard-drive information found?

    _____

    _____

    _____

    _____

3. Which utility displays the system's operating system in DOS?

    _____

    _____

    _____

    _____

    _____

4. What is the function of the IRQ?

    _____

    _____

    _____

    _____

5. How is the I/O address used?

    _____

    _____

    _____

    _____

Lab 6.6: CMOS Setup

System parameters are stored in the CMOS (Complementary Metal Oxide Semiconductor) memory. The most reliable listing of current hard-drive setup information is found in the CMOS settings of a properly configured computer system. In most computers, the BIOS contains a subroutine that permits you to edit the CMOS files and change the system parameters. If a change is made to the computer hardware, or the CMOS loses power, you may need to run the setup routine so the correct values can be placed into the CMOS.

For some older computers, these CMOS setup subroutines are available on a floppy disk rather than as part of the BIOS routine. Utility disks that can edit the CMOS are available. The subroutine in the BIOS itself is usually a better choice, however, because it matches that particular system. Each BIOS manufacturer provides a unique method for starting and running the CMOS setup routine. Some common methods used are F2 or DEL. Here are a few other examples:

AMIBIOS   Boot the computer and press F1, F10, or the Delete key during the boot process.

AWARD BIOS, DTK BIOS, and Mr. BIOS   Press Ctrl+Alt+Esc after the computer has booted.

PHOENIX BIOS   Press Ctrl+Alt+S or Ctrl+Alt+Esc or Ctrl+Alt+J after the computer has booted.

A Plug-and-Play (PnP) BIOS is designed to automatically update the CMOS files. When PnP computers perform their own setup properly, things are easier. But when the PnP does not perform a setup properly, you must be prepared to run the CMOS routine and override the settings.

Upon completion of this lab, you will be able to:

- Run the CMOS setup routine
- Change CMOS data on a computer

Set Up

For this exercise, you will need an operational PC.

Exercise

In this lab, you will run the CMOS setup routine for your computer. One of the previously listed methods may work on your computer, or the correct command may be displayed during the boot process. Sometimes you'll need to check your computer's documentation to find the correct input to run the CMOS routine.

Running the CMOS Setup Routine

To run the CMOS setup routine,

1. Boot the computer.
2. Run the CMOS setup routine for your computer. As you work through it, answer the questions in the rest of this exercise.

3. What type of BIOS is installed?

    _____

4. What procedure is used to run the setup routine?

    _____

5. Record the hard drive information in Table 6.5. If you can't find the hard-drive information in the CMOS, it can often be obtained by pressing the Break key during the startup sequence. The information is often displayed for only a very short period of time, so you must act quickly.

TABLE 6.5   Hard Drive Information

	Drive C:	Drive D:
Type Number	_____	_____
Heads	_____	_____
Cylinders	_____	_____
Sectors	_____	_____
Size	_____	_____

6. Record the floppy-drive information.

    _____

7. Record the date and time as displayed in the CMOS.

    _____

8. Change the date and time to any value. Record the new date and time.

    _____

9. Save the changes and exit the setup routine. Doing so reboots the computer.

10. Run the setup routine again. Is the date displayed the date you entered? Y N

11. Change the date and time to the correct values, save the changes, and exit the setup routine.

Lab Report 6.6

1. What is the function of the CMOS?

_____

_____

_____

_____

2. What determines the method used to run the CMOS setup routine on your computer?

_____

_____

_____

_____

3. Which motherboard component contains the subroutine that runs the CMOS setup?

_____

_____

_____

_____

4. What may cause the CMOS to forget system settings?

_____

_____

_____

_____

_____

Answers to Lab Report 6.1

1. In some computers, a card will not function if it is moved to a different slot unless the card's drivers are reinstalled.
2. An AT type motherboard may be damaged if you reverse the power supply connections.
3. Your sketch may be the only document to show the proper connections.
4. The stripe identifies the pin-1 edge of the cable.

Answers to Lab Report 6.2

1. Store RAM in an antistatic bag and wear antistatic wrist straps when you handle the RAM.
2. Type the MEM command at the command prompt.
3. Usually a computer will not boot unless the lowest-numbered bank is filled.
4. The operating system and open applications are placed into RAM when the computer is booted and the applications are opened.

Answers to Lab Report 6.3

1. The power switch has 120 volts applied to it any time the power cable is attached to an outlet.
2. The motherboard of an ATX computer has 5 volts applied to it any time the power cable is attached to an outlet.
3. The black wires in the power plug are next to each other.
4. The motherboard would probably be damaged.

Answers to Lab Report 6.4

1. When the CD-ROM drive is being installed on the same data cable as the bootable hard drive, the CD-ROM drive is set to slave.
2. Jumpers are provided to select the master or slave position.
3. For best performance, the CD-ROM drive should be installed as the master drive on the secondary IDE interface.
4. The pin-1 edge of the IDE data cable has a stripe.

Answers to Lab Report 6.5

1. The MSD utility displays DOS system resources.

2. The CMOS contains the hard-drive information.

3. The VER command displays the DOS version installed.

4. A device uses an IRQ numbers to alert the processor when it needs service.

5. An I/O address is a location the processor uses to communicate with a particular device. Each device has its own I/O address.

Answers to Lab Report 6.6

1. The CMOS remembers the computer's device information.

2. The sequence used to start the setup routine depends on the BIOS installed in your computer.

3. The system BIOS contains the setup subroutine.

4. CMOS will forget the settings if it loses power. Power may be lost if the battery goes dead or if the battery is momentarily shorted.

Chapter

7

Portable Systems

LABS YOU WILL PERFORM IN THIS CHAPTER:

✓ Lab 7.1: Basic Laptop Maintenance

One of the fastest growing areas of hardware is the realm of portable systems—everything from laptops to handheld computers. Just about everyone today who uses a portable system is using it for access to the Internet and their own convenience. The hardware used in portable systems has made tremendous advances in overcoming size and weight limitations.

The difficulty for the hardware technician is that many of the components used in a laptop are proprietary. Compatibility between laptop manufacturers is somewhat limited.

 For more information, see Chapter 7 of David Groth's *A+ Complete Study Guide* (Sybex, 2003).

Lab 7.1: Basic Laptop Maintenance

A laptop has many of the same connections that a PC has. The main difference between the two is the placement and availability of these connections. Many laptops rely on a docking station to provide the full functionality of a PC. Others have a number of external connections and take advantage of Personal Computer Memory Card International Association (PCMCIA) devices that can readily be plugged into the PCMCIA slots. To fully understand all the slots that are available, you should refer to your owner's manual.

PCMCIA devices are categorized into three types that can be easily identified by their thickness:

- *Type I cards* are 3.3mm thick and are typically used for flash memory.
- *Type II cards* are 5mm thick and are used for I/O devices— modems, LAN connections, and so on.
- *Type III cards* are 10.5mm thick. The most common use for Type III cards is hard drives.

  Upon completion of this lab, you will be able to:

- Describe the external connections on a laptop
- Remove and install Field Replaceable Units (FRU)
- Clean the LCD panel

Specific Safety Issues

The safety of the technician and the computer must be considered when a laptop computer is being repaired or updated.

A laptop is designed to take more shock than a PC; however; you still need to take care not to drop or shock any of the components as you remove them from the laptop.

Before you remove the hard drive, it is a good idea to back up any of the information stored on it if possible. Never remove the hard drive while the system is powered on or in hibernate mode.

Although you can safely remove a PCMCIA card while the system is on, doing so can cause an unexpected error to your programs or the operating system. Many operating systems have an icon representing the device in the Taskbar. By clicking on the device's icon, you can access an option to disable the device/slot before removing it. The same is true for undocking the laptop from a docking station.

A docking station is a common addition for many laptops. The docking station allows the laptop to extend its functionality by providing additional external connectors and a power source. When the laptop is in a docked state, the docking station takes on the function of providing power. Additionally, you will normally have connectors for a monitor, keyboard, mouse, network, and USB. Each manufacturer may have additional options as well.

Set Up

For this exercise you will need a working laptop computer.

Exercise

In this exercise you will identify the external connectors on the laptop. You will also remove and replace the battery and the memory packaging.

Identifying External Connections

To identify external connections:

1. Shut down the laptop computer and turn off the power to all peripherals.

2. Sketch the back of the computer, showing where each cable can be attached.

3. Sketch the sides of the computer, showing where each cable can be attached and where all the slots are.

4. Sketch the underside of the computer, showing where each latch and cover is.

5. Identify all the covers and what is under them.

Remove and Install the Battery Assembly

To remove and install the battery assembly:

1. With the laptop turned off, locate the latches that secure the battery assembly. Release the latches.

2. Slide the battery assembly out of its slot.

3. Inspect the battery and the slot.

4. Replace the battery and ensure the latches lock it back into place.

Remove and Install the Memory Package

To remove and install the memory package:

1. With the laptop turned off, locate the latches that secure the memory access panel. Remove the cover.

When handling memory packages, it is a good idea to also remove the battery and hard drive to prevent any corruption of data or damage from ESD to the drive connectors.

2. Gently slide the memory package out of its slot. Some laptops have clips or locks that hold the memory package in place. Release them first before removing the memory package.

3. Inspect the memory package and the slot.

4. Replace the memory package and ensure that it locks back into place.

5. Replace the access panel.

   To install a PCMCIA memory card:

1. Locate the PCMCIA Type I slot and insert the memory card.

Cleaning an LCD Panel

To clean an LCD panel:

1. Open the laptop to reveal the screen. With the laptop powered off, it is easier to see fingerprints and dirt on the screen.

2. Using a lint-free cloth moistened with water, gently wipe away any fingerprints, smudges, and dirt.

Although most laptop screens can be cleaned with glass cleaner, some screens have a capacitive coating that can be damaged by the glass cleaner. Never spray any liquid directly onto the screen. Droplets from the liquid may cause electrical shorts in the system.

Do not apply excessive pressure while cleaning the LCD panel. It is very easy to crack the screen if too much pressure is applied.

Lab Report 7.1

1. What is the difference between Type I, Type II, and Type III PCMCIA cards?

_____

_____

_____

_____

2. What determines which PCMCIA cards will fit into a laptop?

_____

_____

_____

_____

3. What function does a docking station provide?

_____

_____

_____

_____

Answers to Lab Report 7.1

1. Type I cards are 3.3mm thick and are used for flash memory. Type II cards are 5mm thick and are primarily used for I/O devices. Type III cards are 10.5mm thick and are used for hard drives.

2. The PCMCIA cards that will work with a particular laptop is determined by which type of slots are provided. The number of slots will determine how many cards can be added simultaneously.

3. A docking station adds to the overall functionality of the laptop. It adds a full-size keyboard, a mouse, and full-size monitor. Frequently, it also adds network connectivity and additional ports to connect devices.

Chapter 8

Installing and Upgrading PC Components

LABS YOU WILL PERFORM IN THIS CHAPTER:

- ✓ Lab 8.1: Changing Display Properties and Upgrading Display Drivers
- ✓ Lab 8.2: Installing a Mouse in a DOS System
- ✓ Lab 8.3: Installing and Customizing a Mouse in Windows 98
- ✓ Lab 8.4: Installing a Sound Card in a DOS System
- ✓ Lab 8.5: Installing a Sound Card in Windows 9x

The modular construction of the PC and its ability to accept a wide variety of peripheral devices greatly increase its usefulness. The keyboard is the most important input device, and the monitor is the most important output device.

Input and output devices are software driven by device drivers that must be loaded in order for the devices to function. Device drivers are loaded from the operating system installation software during the installation of the OS or from software supplied by the peripheral manufacturer. If you add any new peripherals after the OS is installed, you must install their device drivers.

Windows provides a Hardware Wizard to assist you with device driver installation. The Hardware Wizard usually gives you an option for using a driver from the OS installation CD or from the peripheral manufacturer. Most of the time, if the manufacturer supplies a driver for a particular peripheral, and the driver is compatible with the OS in use, then that driver is the best choice.

Peripheral devices use system resources, and sometimes a new device creates a conflict with currently installed devices. A device conflict may cause the computer to malfunction until the conflict is removed. Windows provides the Device Manager to manage the computer's devices.

For more information, see Chapter 8 of David Groth's *A+ Complete Study Guide* (Sybex, 2003).

Lab 8.1: Changing Display Properties and Upgrading Display Drivers

The video adapter (video card) is the key to better picture quality. Speed is the dominant feature of video cards. Higher speed permits faster screen refreshes and therefore better video motion. The monitor must have sufficient resolution to support the newer video cards. If the monitor doesn't support the faster speeds or resolution, you will have to set the video card for a lesser speed or resolution. (SVGA has 1024 × 768 resolution). The product of the resolution numbers is the number of *pixels* (picture elements) available on the screen. The larger the number of pixels, the better the picture quality.

Monitors are classed according to their resolution and the number of colors they support. VGA monitors have a maximum resolution of 640 × 480 with 16 colors, SVGA monitors have a maximum resolution of 1024 × 768 with 16 colors, and XVGA monitors have a maximum resolution of 1024 × 768 with 256 colors.

Upon completion of this lab, you will be able to:

- Examine current display properties
- Change display properties

Set Up

For this lab you, will need an operational PC with Windows 9x installed.

Exercise

In this lab, you will use the Display Properties dialog box to examine and modify the display settings.

Changing the Display Properties

1. Boot the computer and right-click any empty area on the Desktop. Carefully observe the screen colors, window size, and screen flicker.

2. When the menu is displayed, click Properties.

3. Select the Settings tab.

4. Select Advanced and then click Adapter. The video adapter information is displayed. This is the information needed for an Internet search for the video driver. Record the manufacturer of the display adapter:

    _____

    Record the model number (if available):

    _____

5. Click Close to close the Video Card Properties window. The Display section shows the color scheme and the screen resolution. Record the current values:

    Color Scheme (Colors in Windows 98):

    _____

    Screen Resolution (Screen Area in Windows 98):

    _____

    Changes to these values could cause problems. If you have a record of the correct values, returning the system to normal is easier.

6. Select a new screen resolution by sliding the Resolution bar to the left or right while you observe the changes in the sample display window.

7. Click the following sequence to accept the new settings:

    Apply ➢ OK ➢ Yes

    The computer may need to reboot if you want to observe the new settings.

8. Reboot to the Desktop if necessary, and compare the Desktop with the observation in step 1.

9. Set the screen resolution back to its original value. (See steps 1 through 6.)

10. Reboot to the Desktop if necessary, and compare the Desktop with the observation in step 1.

11. Right-click any empty area on the Desktop.

12. When the menu is displayed, select Properties.

13. Select the Settings tab in the Display Properties dialog box.

14. Change the color scheme by clicking the Colors drop-down menu to show the color options and then clicking the desired option.

15. Click the following sequence to accept the new settings:

    Apply ➢ OK ➢ Yes

16. Return to the Desktop and observe the changes.

17. Use the Display Properties dialog box to set the maximum colors and maximum screen resolution. Record the highest values the system permits:

    Colors:

    _____

    Screen Area:

    _____

    If the display becomes unreadable, boot in Safe mode and change the settings to usable values. If the display does not occupy the entire screen, you have exceeded the maximum settings.

    What type of video adapter is indicated by the display's performance? (Circle one.)
    VGA   SVGA   XVGA

 If the Windows default drivers are used for an XVGA video adapter, the actual performance is VGA level; therefore, it is important to use the proper driver. You may need to consider upgrading the video driver.

18. Change the resolution and color scheme back to the original settings.

Upgrading the Display Driver

1. Boot the computer to the Desktop, and follow this sequence:

    Start ➤ Settings ➤ Control Panel ➤ Add New Hardware

2. Click Next.

3. When you see the prompt *Do you want Windows to search for your new hardware?*, click No.

4. Click Next.

5. Choose Display Adapters.

6. Click Next.

7. Click Have Disk.

8. Insert the display adapter driver disk.

9. Choose the drive that contains the driver, click Next, and follow the prompts.

10. Boot the computer and return to "Changing the Display Properties" at the beginning of this lab for instructions for setting the display properties.

Lab Report 8.1

1. What is the maximum resolution for a VGA adapter?

    _____

    _____

2. If the picture occupies less than full screen, what is likely to be the problem?

    _____

    _____

3. If you use the Windows default video driver instead of the manufacturer's driver, what level of operation can you expect from the video adapter?

    _____

    _____

4. If the display becomes unreadable after you make a change, how do you solve the problem?

_____

_____

Lab 8.2: Installing a Mouse in a DOS System

The mouse is one of the first pieces of hardware to be added to a computer. Whether you are installing a mouse or some other piece of hardware, the process is very much the same. You must determine the system resources, physically install the device, configure the computer, and then test the hardware item you installed.

Upon completion of this lab, you will be able to install a serial mouse in a DOS system.

Set Up

For this exercise, you will need:

- A working PC with DOS installed
- A serial mouse
- A mouse driver
- A DOS utility disk

Exercise

In this lab, you will determine the COM port IRQ assignments, install a serial mouse, install a mouse driver, and observe the changes in the AUTOEXEC.BAT file when a mouse driver is installed.

Installing the Mouse

1. Boot the computer and determine the COM port IRQ assignments by using the MSD command:

    C:\>**MSD**

    Record the COM port IRQ numbers:

    _____

2. Shut down the computer, plug the mouse into an unused serial port, and then boot the computer.

3. To display the AUTOEXEC.BAT file, enter the following command:

    `C:\>`**`TYPE AUTOEXEC.BAT`**

    Copy the AUTOEXEC.BAT file into the space provided:

    _____

    _____

    _____

    _____

4. To display the CONFIG.SYS file, enter the following command:

    `C:\>`**`TYPE CONFIG.SYS`**

    Copy the CONFIG.SYS file into the space:

    _____

    _____

    _____

    _____

5. To find the mouse installation program, insert the mouse driver disk and enter the following:

    `A:\>`**`DIR`**

    In the directory that is displayed, look for a file that contains `Install` or `Setup`.

6. To install the mouse driver, enter the installation filename. Accept all defaults:

    `A:\>`**`INSTALL`**

7. Reboot the computer. The boot process executes the changes made to the AUTOEXEC.BAT and CONFIG.SYS files by the mouse driver.

8. To test the mouse, execute the EDIT program or any program that supports a mouse:

    `C:\>`**`EDIT`**

9. To exit the EDIT utility, click FILE, and then click EXIT.

10. If the mouse does not function, press Alt+F to open a menu, press the X key to exit the Edit utility, and then return to step 6.

11. Compare the AUTOEXEC.BAT and CONFIG.SYS files with the originals from steps 3 and 4. Enter the following to display the files:

    C:\>TYPE AUTOEXEC.BAT
    C:\>TYPE CONFIG.SYS

12. Run the MSD utility and note the mouse port and the IRQ assignment for the mouse port:

    C:\>MSD

Lab Report 8.2

1. When is the mouse active in a DOS system?

    _____

    _____

2. What is the function of the MSD utility?

    _____

    _____

3. Why must you reboot the computer after the mouse driver is installed?

    _____

    _____

4. If you are in a program such as EDIT and the mouse does not function, how do you return to the DOS prompt?

    _____

    _____

Lab 8.3: Installing and Customizing a Mouse in Windows 98

The mouse is a critical part of any GUI operating system. If it is attached in an operational port before power is applied to the computer, Windows will usually find the mouse and make it active; however, the mouse will use the Windows driver and may not have all of its features active. A mouse with special features has its own driver, which must be installed.

Upon completion of this lab, you will be able to:

- Install a mouse in a Windows system
- Customize the mouse

Set Up

For this exercise, you will need a working PC with Windows 98 installed and a mouse that can be installed. If the mouse has special functions, you will need the mouse driver.

Exercise

In this lab, you will install a mouse in a Windows system and customize that mouse.

Installing the Mouse

To install the mouse, follow these steps:

1. If the computer is running, use the normal shutdown procedure. If the mouse is not functioning, you can use the following procedure to shut down the computer: Press Alt+F4 to close an open program, press Ctrl+Esc to open the Start menu, and then press the appropriate underlined letter in each of the following displays to complete the shutdown.

2. Locate the serial port and attach the mouse.

3. Boot the computer to Windows 98. The mouse should be operational. If the mouse needs a driver for its special functions, Windows may ask for the driver. If the driver is requested, follow the on-screen instructions.

4. If the mouse driver is not requested and the special functions are not available, use the Add New Hardware feature to install the mouse driver:

    Start ➤ Settings ➤Control Panel ➤ Add New Hardware

5. When the New Hardware Wizard opens, click Next and then click Next again to have Windows search for the new mouse.

6. When a device list is displayed, select No, the Device Isn't on the List and then click Next.

7. When prompted, select No, I Want to Select Hardware from the List and then click Next.

8. In the list provided, select Mouse and then click Next.

9. When the manufacturer's list is displayed, select Have Disk and follow instructions.

Customizing the Mouse

To customize the mouse, follow these steps:

1. The following sequence opens the Mouse dialog box and permits you to make modifications to the mouse:

      My Computer ➤ Control Panel ➤ Mouse

2. The Mouse dialog box has three tabs. Each tab provides access to different mouse characteristics:

   - The Motion tab lets you select the pointer speed and provides mouse-trail options.

   - The Pointer tab lets you select the pointer shape.

   - The Buttons tab lets you select the mouse button functions and the double-click speed. Left-handed users often want to change the mouse-button functions.

   Make some changes to the mouse and observe the differences in operation.

Lab Report 8.3

1. Will having the wrong mouse driver installed cause some of the mouse features to function while other mouse features do not function?

   _____

   _____

2. What sequence opens the Mouse dialog box and permits you to change the mouse-pointer speed?

   _____

   _____

3. How would you change the mouse buttons to accommodate a left-handed person?

   _____

   _____

4. If the mouse does not function, how do you shut down the computer?

_____

_____

_____

Lab 8.4: Installing a Sound Card in a DOS System

Sound cards are used to convert electronic signals into electrical signals that a speaker can convert into sound. This lab presents the process of installing a sound card in a DOS computer. Sound cards tend to be difficult to configure because they often produce resource conflicts with other hardware devices. These conflicts often cause other peripherals to malfunction.

Upon completion of this lab, you will be able to install a sound card in a DOS system.

Set Up

For this exercise, you will need:

- A working DOS system
- A sound card and its DOS driver
- An audio CD-ROM disk
- An audio cable for the CD-ROM drive
- A speaker
- A DOS utility disk

Exercise

In this lab, you will determine which IRQs (interrupt requests) are available for new devices, set the sound card jumpers to an available IRQ, install the sound card, and then configure the system by installing a sound card driver.

Installing the Sound Card

To install the sound card, follow these steps:

1. Boot the computer and run the MSD utility to display the IRQ assignments:

C:\>**MSD**

2. Set the IRQ jumper on the sound card to an unused IRQ. Some Plug-and-Play sound cards may not have jumpers, and the sound card driver software assigns the IRQ automatically.

3. Disconnect all cables from the back of the computer.

4. Remove the computer cover.

5. Route the audio cable through the CD-ROM drive bay and attach it to the CD-ROM drive.

6. Insert the sound card into an expansion slot and attach the audio cable to the sound card.

   Do not move the CD-ROM data cable to the sound card if it has a CD-ROM drive interface. Doing so will change the master/slave status of both the hard drive and the CD-ROM drive.

7. Close the cover, reattach the cables to the back of the computer, and reboot.

8. Insert the sound card driver disk into drive A: and enter **SETUP** at the A: prompt to install the sound card driver:

   A:\>SETUP

9. Follow the prompts and reboot the computer.

10. To test the sound card, attach a speaker, insert an audio CD-ROM disk, and access the disk. The following command assumes that drive D: is the CD-ROM drive:

    C:\>D:

11. If you can hear the sounds produced by the computer, the sound card is operational. If you can't hear the sounds, check for resource conflicts.

Lab Report 8.4

1. Why did you leave the CD-ROM drive connected to the hard drive controller?

_____

_____

_____

2. Which utility displays the IRQ assignments?

_____

_____

_____

3. What is the likely problem if one of your peripherals malfunctions after the sound card is installed?

_____

_____

_____

4. Why does the computer require a sound card driver?

_____

_____

_____

_____

Lab 8.5: Installing a Sound Card in Windows 9x

This lab introduces the process of installing a sound card in a computer with a Windows 9x operating system. Sound cards tend to be difficult to configure because they often produce resource conflicts with other hardware devices. Many of the sound cards available today are Plug-and-Play. When these cards are installed in a Windows 9x system, they are automatically configured and set up with the appropriate resources. When Plug-and-Play fails to properly configure the computer, you may need to manually assign resources and manually install drivers. This procedure can be adapted to the installation of other hardware items.

Upon completion of this lab, you will be able to install a sound card in a Windows 9x computer.

Set Up

For this exercise, you will need:

- A working Windows 9x computer
- A sound card
- A CD-ROM audio cable
- A speaker
- A sound card driver
- A Windows 9x installation CD

Exercise

Because the normal installation process often fails to work, both the normal installation process and the manual installation process for installing a sound card are shown in this lab.

Installing the Sound Card

To install the sound card, follow these steps:

1. Disconnect all external cables from the computer and remove the computer cover.

2. Find an open expansion slot and insert the sound card into the space.

3. Attach the sound cable to the CD audio connector on the sound card and to the CD-ROM drive.

 Do not move the CD-ROM data cable to the sound card if it has a CD-ROM drive interface. If you do, the master/slave status of both the hard drive and the CD-ROM drive will change.

4. Install the speakers on the audio out port on the back of the sound card.

5. Reconnect the external cables and boot the computer. If Windows 9x correctly identifies the sound card, it will install the appropriate drivers. Windows may ask for the installation CD-ROM during this process so the appropriate driver can be loaded. After the computer has reached the Windows Desktop, you should hear the Windows Startup sound.

6. Follow this sequence to test the sound card after the computer has booted:

    Start ➤ Settings ➤ Control Panel ➤ Sounds

7. From the section of the window labeled Events, choose an event with a yellow speaker beside it. Highlight the event.

8. Below, next to Preview, select the arrow to test for sound. If the installation was a success, you should hear the sound.

9. If you don't hear a sound, verify that Windows Default is selected in Schemes.

10. If Windows did not find the new hardware, use the Add New Hardware Wizard to install the hardware item.

11. Close all programs.

12. Use the following sequence, and accept the defaults:

    Start ➢ Settings ➢ Control Panel ➢ Add New Hardware

13. Reboot. The new hardware should be operational. Follow the instructions in steps 3 and 4 to test the sound card.

If the computer incorrectly identified the sound card or there is a conflict with other hardware, you'll see yellow question marks (?) or red exclamation marks (!) in Device Manager. These conflict indicators appear in the Sound, Video, and Game Controller area and/or in the Other Devices area of Device Manager. Sometimes, yellow question marks (?) appear on items that appear to be functioning normally. All conflict indicators that refer to the sound card must be removed before you can use another method to install the sound card:

1. Boot to Normal or Safe mode and use the following sequence to display Device Manager:

    Start ➢ Settings ➢ Control Panel ➢ System ➢ Device Manager

2. If you see yellow question marks or red exclamation marks in front of the Sound, Video, and Game Controller and/or Other Device entries in Device Manager, use the following steps to remove the entries.

3. Click the plus sign (+) next to the item that has a question mark or exclamation mark to expand that item.

4. Click to highlight a reference to the sound card or joystick ports in these expanded folders, and then click Remove. Repeat this process for each entry.

5. Click OK to close this window after you are finished.

6. Use the manual procedure to install the sound card.

Manually Installing a Sound Card

1. Boot the computer to the Desktop and follow this sequence:

    Start ➢ Settings ➢ Control Panel ➢ Add New Hardware

2. Click Next.

3. When you see the prompt *Do you want Windows to search for your new hardware?*, choose No.

4. Click Next.

5. Choose Sound, Video, and Game Controllers.

6. Click Next.

7. Click Have Disk.

8. Insert the sound card driver disk.

9. Choose your sound card from the menu and follow the prompts. You may need to use the Windows installation CD during the process.

10. If you are prompted for the pathname in the Copying Files window, enter

    D:\WIN98

    where **D:** represents the CD-ROM drive letter.

11. Boot the computer. At the Windows Desktop, you should hear the startup sound. If the sound does not play, follow this sequence to test the sound:

    Start ➢ Settings ➢ Control Panel ➢ Sounds

12. From the section of the window labeled Events, choose an event with a yellow speaker beside it. Highlight the event.

13. Below, next to Preview, select the arrow to test for sound. If the installation was a success, you should hear the sound.

Lab Report 8.5

1. Why did you leave the CD-ROM drive connected to the hard drive controller?

   _____

   _____

   _____

2. If colored punctuation marks are found in Device Manager, what is indicated?

   _____

   _____

   _____

3. Give a procedure for testing a sound card.

_____

_____

_____

4. Which window displays IRQ conflicts?

_____

_____

Answers to Lab Reports

Lab Report 8.1

1. The maximum resolution for a VGA monitor is 640×480.

2. The resolution is set too high for the system as it is configured.

3. The video resolution for the Windows default video driver is VGA.

4. Boot to Safe mode and change the settings back.

Lab Report 8.2

1. The mouse is active when you open a program that supports a mouse.

2. It displays system information.

3. The rebooting process executes the changes the mouse installation made in the AUTOEXEC.BAT and CONFIG.SYS files.

4. Press Alt+F to open the drop-down menu, and then press the X key.

Lab Report 8.3

1. Yes. Mice with special features require a special driver.

2. Use the following sequence to open the mouse dialog box: Start ➢ Settings ➢ Control Panel ➢ Mouse.

3. To change the button functions, go to the Button tab in the mouse properties dialog box.

4. If the mouse is not functioning, you press Alt+F4 to close an open program, press Ctrl+Esc to open the Start menu, and then press the appropriate underlined letter in each of the following displays to complete the shutdown.

Lab Report 8.4

1. Moving the CD-ROM data cable to the sound card can change the master/slave status of other drives in the system.

2. The MSD utility displays the IRQ assignments and other system information.

3. Sound cards often create resource conflicts when they are installed. These conflicts can cause problems for the sound card and other peripherals.

4. The sound card is a peripheral device, and peripheral devices require a device driver (software) to function.

Lab Report 8.5

1. Moving the CD-ROM data cable to the sound card could cause problems with drive identification.

2. Colored punctuations marks in Device Manager indicate a resource conflict.

3. In Control Panel, select Sounds, choose an event that has a yellow speaker, and then click Preview.

4. Resource conflicts are displayed in Device Manager.

Chapter

9

Optimizing PC Performance and Preventative Maintenance

LABS YOU WILL PERFORM IN THIS CHAPTER:

✓ **Lab 9.1: Cleaning Computer Components**

Most of us hate doing housework. Yet one of the easiest ways to ensure that our computers stay at peak performance is to do a bit of regular cleaning inside the case. Dust and dirt act as insulators. The buildup of dust inside the computer prevents the system from cooling properly. This situation definitely affects performance and the longevity of the components.

> For more information, see Chapter 9 of David Groth's *A+ Complete Study Guide* (Sybex, 2003).

Lab 9.1: Cleaning Computer Components

Properly cleaning a computer and its peripheral components can decrease strain on the user and the computer components. Fingerprints on a monitor increase glare and eyestrain, leading to user discomfort. Buildup of dirt in the mouse causes it to act sporadically, causing user frustration. In general, keeping your equipment clean is one of the first steps of preventative maintenance and of optimizing your computer.

Upon completion of this lab, you will be able to:

- Properly clean dust from the system

- Properly clean a mouse

- Properly clean a keyboard

- Properly clean CDs and CD-ROM drives

- Properly clean the computer case and monitor

Set Up

To complete this lab, you will need a working computer, a soft cloth, rubbing alcohol, and a can of compressed air or a computer vacuum.

Exercises

The simplest type of computer maintenance is periodic cleaning. Eliminating dust buildup inside the computer can help keep it running. Removing dirt and fingerprints from a monitor reduces eyestrain. Cleaning the keyboard and mouse improves their performance.

Dusting Computer Components

To dust computer components,

1. Turn off the computer and open the case. You may want to do this in an area where you won't mind dust blowing around.

2. Use either compressed air or a vacuum to clean the dust from the motherboard, CPU fan, system fan, and other components. If you're using compressed air, makes sure you direct the air so that it blows the dust out of the case.

Be careful to hold the can of compressed air upright. If the can is tilted, it may spray out chemicals that can cause corrosion on the motherboard and other components.

If you use a computer vacuum, make sure you keep the nozzle a couple of inches above the motherboard to prevent accidental contact. Ensure that the vacuum doesn't suck up small components, including jumpers, small screws, and so on.

You can purchase small computer vacuums that don't create ESD and that don't generate enough suction to suck up small components. Do not use a regular vacuum to clean the inside of the computer.

3. Close the computer case.

Cleaning a Mechanical Mouse

To clean a mechanical mouse,

1. Unplug the mouse from the computer.
2. Turn the mouse over. Remove the mouse cover by twisting the cover one-eighth of a turn counterclockwise.
3. Place your hand under the mouse and tilt the mouse to remove the cover and mouse ball.
4. You can clean the mouse ball with a mild detergent and warm water. Make sure the mouse ball is dry before you insert it into the mouse.
5. Look inside the mouse housing. You can see the mouse rollers inside. There may be a buildup of dirt and hair on the rollers. Use your finger or fingernail to remove as much of the dirt buildup as possible. Tip the mouse over and gently shake it to get the debris out of the housing.
6. Once the housing is cleaned out and the mouse ball is dry, insert the mouse ball into the housing. Replace the cover and twist it one-eighth of a turn clockwise until it locks into place.
7. Plug the cleaned mouse back into the computer.

Cleaning an Optical Mouse

To clean an optical mouse,

1. Unplug the mouse from the computer.

2. Turn the mouse over. You will notice a port that is used by the light source to detect motion. This port frequently catches hair and other debris. You can remove the debris by gently blowing so it becomes dislodged. Alternatively, you can remove the debris by wiping down the surface.

3. Plug the cleaned mouse back into the computer.

Cleaning Dust and Debris from a Keyboard

To clean dust and debris from a keyboard,

1. Unplug the keyboard from the computer.

2. Turn the keyboard upside down and shake it. Doing so dislodges loose debris and hair from the keyboard.

3. Using compressed air, direct the air between the keys to blow away dust and debris. A vacuum cleaner can be used to suck up debris. Be careful not to suck up any loose keys.

Cleaning Liquids from a Keyboard

To clean out any liquid that has been spilled onto the keyboard,

1. Unplug the keyboard immediately. Turn the keyboard upside down over a sink or other area where the liquid will not cause problems.

2. Use a cloth or paper towel to wipe away as much of the liquid as possible. You can then use distilled, demineralized water to rinse away the residue from the keyboard.

3. Allow the keyboard to dry overnight or longer before plugging it into the computer.

Cleaning CDs and CD-ROM Drives

Follow these steps for cleaning CDs and CD-ROM drives:

1. To clean a CD-ROM drive, purchase a CD-ROM cleaning kit form any computer store. Regular use of the kit should keep the drive functioning properly. Take measures to prevent accidental insertion of foreign objects into the drive, such as cups, sandwiches, and so on.

2. To clean a CD, wipe it using a soft cloth; wipe from the center outward, going against the tracks. Do not wipe in a circular motion; doing so can create problems with reading the CD. For stubborn substances on the CD, try using a little rubbing alcohol or glass cleaner.

Cleaning the Computer Case and Monitor

To clean the computer case and monitor,

1. Unplug the computer. Use a soft cloth to dust the surface of the case. Pay attention to the ventilation holes. Wipe off the dust to keep the air circulating properly. For any stubborn stains, use a cloth that has been dampened with a bit of water. You can use a cloth dampened with soapy water for the really tough stains. Do not use any cleaning solvents on the case; these generally cause stains in the plastic that cannot be removed.

2. Clean the monitor screen using glass cleaner. Be sure to spray the glass cleaner onto a soft cloth and not directly onto the monitor. Doing so prevents the glass cleaner from accidentally being sprayed onto the electronics inside the case.

3. Clean the monitor case using the same procedure listed in step 1.

Lab Report 9.1

1. What should you use to clean dust from the motherboard and other internal components?

_____

_____

_____

_____

2. Why should you never spray cleaner onto a computer or monitor?

_____

_____

_____

_____

3. Why do you need to clean the mouse?

_____

_____

_____

_____

4.   Why shouldn't you use circular motions when cleaning a CD?

_____

_____

_____

_____

Answers to Lab Report 9.1

1. You should use compressed air or a vacuum designed for use on computers to clean the dust from the motherboard and other internal components.

2. Spraying cleaner or water onto a computer can cause the components to short themselves out, thus causing permanent damage to the computer.

3. Dirt and hair tend to build up inside a mouse, decreasing the mouse's responsiveness.

4. Circular motions can cause more damage to the surface of a CD. You should clean from the inside to the outside edge of the CD.

Chapter

10

Hardware Troubleshooting

LABS YOU WILL PERFORM IN THIS CHAPTER:

- ✓ Lab 10.1: Using a Multimeter
- ✓ Lab 10.2: Creating a Boot Disk
- ✓ Lab 10.3: Booting to Safe Mode

In this chapter, we will cover some basic tools used in troubleshooting a computer. The first tool we will discuss is the multimeter. This tool can help ensure that the proper voltages are delivered to a device. If the wrong voltage is applied, the device may be overworked or not have enough power to function properly.

Next we will discuss how to create a boot disk. A good boot disk lets you gain access to a system, should the boot files become corrupt. Many issues can be resolved after the system can be booted properly.

The last tool we'll explore is included with the Windows operating systems. Safe mode is a mode of operation that includes only the minimum devices needed to get the system working. Once in the system, you have the ability to enable or disable devices. You can also uninstall or update device drivers. After you have made the appropriate changes to the system, you should be able to boot normally.

For more information, see Chapter 10 of David Groth's *A+ Study Guide* (Sybex, 2003).

Lab 10.1: Using a Multimeter

A multimeter is an invaluable tool when it comes to ensuring that the correct voltages are being passed to a device or computer. It helps you determine whether the problems you may be experiencing are the result of faulty power or a faulty device. If the proper voltages are not being delivered, the devices cannot function properly.

You can also use a multimeter to perform continuity checks on cables. A continuity check gives you a quick indication of whether a wire is broken. If you get a reading of 0 ohms, the wire is good. If the reading is infinite, there is a break in the cable. The same check can be performed on a fuse to see if it is still good.

Upon completion of this lab, you will be able to:

- Use a multimeter to measure DC voltages
- Use a multimeter to perform a continuity check

Set Up

For this lab, you will need the following:

- A working computer
- A multimeter with leads
- An IDE cable

Exercises

A multimeter is a very useful tool to help you identify the voltages that are being provided to your computer and peripheral devices.

Measuring DC Voltage on a Molex Connector

To measure DC voltage on a Molex connector,

1. Prepare the multimeter for use. If the multimeter has detachable leads, connect the black lead to the negative jack and the red lead to the positive jack on the multimeter. Set the multimeter to measure DC voltages. Set the meter to read for voltages less than 20VDC.

2. Turn off the computer and unplug it.

3. Remove the system cover.

4. Locate a Molex power connector. It will have two black wires, one red wire, and one yellow wire. The black wires are ground wires. You will determine the voltage carried on the red and yellow wires.

5. Connect the black multimeter lead to one of the black wires and the red multimeter lead to the red wire.

6. Plug in the computer and turn on the power. Observe the voltage reading and record it:

    Red wire voltage:

    _____

7. Turn off the computer and unplug it.

8. Leave the black multimeter lead connected to a black wire. Move the red multimeter lead to the yellow wire.

9. Plug in the computer and turn on the power. Observe the voltage reading and record it:

    Yellow wire voltage:

    _____

10. Turn off the computer and unplug it.

Measuring Continuity

To measure continuity,

1. If you have an extra IDE cable, you can use it; otherwise remove an IDE cable from your computer. Note the location of pin 1 on both the IDE controller on the motherboard and on the IDE devices.

2. Change the setting on the multimeter to read Ohms.

3. Place one lead on one end of pin 1 and the other lead at the other end of pin 1. Record the reading:

_____

Pin 1 reading:

_____

4. If you removed the IDE cable, replace it in the computer. Take care to ensure that pin 1 is connected to pin 1 on the IDE controller on the motherboard and to the pin 1 on the IDE device.

Lab Report 10.1

1. What voltage should you see on the red wire of a Molex power connector?

_____

_____

_____

_____

2. What voltage should you see on the yellow wire of a Molex power connector?

_____

_____

_____

_____

3. What voltage should you see on the yellow wire of a mini power connector?

_____

_____

_____

_____

4. What is the hazard of power sags or other variations in frequency?

_____

_____

_____

_____

5. What is a solution to power surges and sags?

_____

_____

_____

_____

Lab 10.2: Creating a Boot Disk

One of the tools that every PC technician needs is a boot disk that will allow you to boot up the system. Doing so lets you see whether problems you are having are hardware or software related. When you have a boot disk, it is possible to remove devices until the malfunctioning device can be isolated and repaired.

Upon completion of this lab, you will be able to:

- Create a DOS boot disk
- Create a Windows 2000 boot disk

Set Up

For this lab's first exercise, you will need a working computer running Windows 98 and the Windows 98 CD. The second exercise requires a computer running Windows 2000.

Exercises

Each operating system has its own way to create a boot disk. In this lab, you will see how to create one in Windows 98 and in Windows 2000. Windows XP uses the same procedure as Windows 2000 to create its boot disk.

Creating a DOS Boot Disk

To create a DOS boot disk,

1. Label a diskette **Windows 98 boot disk**.

2. Start Windows 98.

3. Use the following sequence to get to the Startup Disk tab:

    Start ➤ Settings ➤ Control Panel ➤ Add/Remove Programs ➤ Startup Disk tab

4. Insert the floppy diskette in the floppy drive and the Windows 98 CD in the CD-ROM drive.

5. Click the Create Disk button.

6. Click OK when the prompt tells you to insert a diskette.

7. Click Finish when the diskette is completed.

8. Shut down the computer and reboot using the diskette to test it.

9. After the test, remove the diskette.

Creating a Windows 2000 Boot Disk

To create a Windows 2000 boot disk,

1. Label a diskette **Windows 2000 boot disk**.

2. Start Windows 2000.

3. Insert the floppy diskette in the floppy drive.

4. Open My Computer and right-click the A: drive.

5. Select Format from the context-sensitive menu.

 The floppy must be formatted with the Windows 2000 Format utility in order for the diskette to be used as a boot disk.

6. Perform a Quick Format on the floppy diskette. Click Close when the format is complete.

7. From the My Computer window, open the C: drive.

8. Follow this sequence:

    Select Tools ➤ Folder Options ➤ View tab

9. To create the boot disk, you need to copy hidden system files from the C: drive to a floppy. Because these files are hidden, you need to unhide them. Under Hidden Files, select the Show Hidden Files option. Uncheck the Hide File Extension for Known File Types option and the Hide System Files option.

10. Click OK to allow the Hide System Files Option to take effect.

11. Click OK to close the Folder Options window.

12. Copy the following files to the diskette: NTLDR, BOOT.INI, and NTDETECT.COM.

> If you are using SCSI controllers for the hard drive, you need to copy the NTBOOTDD.SYS file as well.

13. Shut down the computer and reboot using the diskette to test it.

Lab Report 10.2

1. Where is the Create Disk button located in Windows 98?

    _____

    _____

    _____

    _____

2. What options are you given when you use the Windows 98 boot disk?

    _____

    _____

    _____

    _____

3. What must you do before you copy files to the Windows 2000 boot disk?

_____

_____

_____

_____

4. What files must be copied to the Windows 2000 boot disk?

_____

_____

_____

_____

Lab 10.3: Booting to Safe Mode

Windows 98/2000/XP have a mode of operation that helps you troubleshoot devices. This mode is Safe mode. It is designed to boot the system with only the minimum number of devices operational, which can help you determine if the problems you are having are software related or related to a device.

In Safe mode, Windows uses some basic default settings that load the minimum device drivers necessary to load Windows. You get a mouse pointer, and video starts in VGA mode with 16 colors and 640 × 480 screen resolution. You do not have access to CD-ROM drives, the network, printers, or other devices. To access Safe mode, press F8 after the power on self-test (POST) process.

Windows does give you some options for Safe mode, including starting Safe mode with network support and Safe mode with command-prompt support. These options let you access key driver files if they are located on the network.

Windows 2000/XP add the ability to use the last known good configuration, which is a saved configuration that was used during the last successful boot. This option is very useful when the reason you need to get into Safe mode is to undo a configuration change that is now preventing you from a successful boot.

Windows XP adds a system restore mode that allows you to create restore points. Another feature added to Windows XP is driver rollback. If you need to remove a driver that is affecting the proper operation of the system, you can use Device Manager to roll back the driver.

Upon completion of this lab, you will be able to boot the computer into Safe mode.

Set Up

For this lab, you will need a working computer running Windows 98, Windows 2000, or Windows XP.

Exercise

1. Boot the computer using Windows 98. After POST completes and during the time when Windows is starting, press F8.

2. Record the options for Safe mode:

_____

_____

3. Repeat these steps to boot into Windows 2000 and Windows XP. Record the options:

_____

_____

_____

_____

Lab Report 10.3

1. What drivers are loaded in Safe mode?

_____

_____

_____

_____

2. What options are also available in the Safe mode menu for Windows 98?

_____

_____

_____

_____

3. What options are also available in the Safe mode menu for Windows 2000 Professional?

_____

_____

_____

_____

4. How can you remove a device driver after it has been installed?

_____

_____

_____

_____

Answers to Lab Reports

Lab Report 10.1

1. The red wire should have +5 volts.
2. The yellow wire should have +12 volts.
3. The yellow wire should have +12 volts.
4. Power sags can damage many of the components in the computer. Just as a power surge can cause devices to overwork and overheat, a power sag can cause a hard drive to slow down and operate outside of its normal conditions.
5. An uninterruptible power supply (UPS).

Lab Report 10.2

1. You create a boot disk in the Add/Remove Programs applet in Control Panel.
2. You can start Windows 98 with or without CD-ROM support. You can also look at the Help files.
3. You must format the diskette using the Windows 2000 Format utility.
4. You need to copy the NTLDR, BOOT.INI, and NTDETECT.COM files to the diskette.

Lab Report 10.3

1. Only the minimum drivers to load the system.
2. Safe Mode with Networking and Safe Mode with Command Prompt.
3. Safe Mode with Networking, Safe Modes with Command Prompt Support, and Last Known Good Configuration.
4. Use the Driver Rollback feature in Device Manager.

Chapter 11

Using the Microsoft Windows GUI

LABS YOU WILL PERFORM IN THIS CHAPTER:

✓ **Lab 11.1: Starting Up, Navigating, and Shutting Down a Windows System**

✓ **Lab 11.2: Customizing the Windows Desktop**

✓ **Lab 11.3: Using Files and Folders**

✓ **Lab 11.4: Installing and Launching Applications**

The graphical user interface (GUI) allows the user to select files, programs, or commands by pointing to pictorial representations on the screen rather than having to recall complicated commands with confusing syntax. The Desktop is the central element of the Windows user interface; all operations start and end at the Desktop.

The Start menu provides a pathway to virtually all programs and features of the operating system. It presents multiple options, and when you pick one, it often leads you to additional options. Navigating the Start menu in Windows is basically a process of choosing options until you reach your destination. Sometimes, the difficult part is remembering which options take you where you want to go. It takes practice to learn where the various tools and applications hide. To simplify this task, many users create shortcuts on the Desktop for the applications and tools they use frequently. Then, all you need to do is double-click on the shortcut icon to open the desired program.

In this chapter, we'll cover both the command-line and GUI interfaces. Because the test covers some commands, you need to be comfortable with using the command-line interface. Many times it's easier to perform tasks from the command line rather than use the GUI. In fact, some tools do not have a GUI equivalent, so you are forced to use the command line. So, we'll discuss the command-line interface, which allows you to operate the computer in a DOS-like mode if you need to. In command-line mode, remember that all commands must be typed with the correct spelling and syntax.

Although the GUIs for Windows 9x and Windows 2000/XP are much alike, there are some differences that we'll note.

For more information on using the Windows interface, see Chapter 12 of David Groth's *A+ Complete Study Guide* (Sybex, 2003).

Lab 11.1: Starting Up, Navigating, and Shutting Down a Windows System

In this lab, we'll go over the basic tasks involved in using a Windows 9x/2000/XP operating system. Although these operating systems are very similar, you need to be aware of some major differences. Differences in the GUI are not usually a problem for experienced users, but occasionally they present minor concerns. Remember that help is available in all versions of Windows to provide detailed information on each command.

Upon completion of this lab, you will be able to:

- Start up or *boot* a Windows operating system
- Navigate Windows menus
- Shut down a Windows operating system
- Start, navigate, and exit a command-line session

Set Up

For this lab, you will need a working PC with Windows installed. It is best if you can boot into Windows 98, Windows 2000, and Windows XP to notice the variations between the operating systems. The operating systems have many similarities but also many differences.

 Windows computers have difficulty booting if they are not shut down properly. This lab describes the startup, navigation, and proper shutdown procedures for Windows computers. Both the mouse and keyboard techniques are addressed.

Exercises

Select and perform the procedures that match your operating system.

Starting Up Windows

To start up Windows,

1. Turn on the computer. During the boot process, pay particular attention to any on-screen messages and follow their instructions.

 Windows 9x runs ScanDisk after an improper shutdown. Windows 2000/XP runs the CHKDSK program after an improper shutdown. When these programs run, you usually should accept the defaults and allow any damaged files to be repaired.

2. If a Log On window appears, enter the username and password. If there is no password, click OK. The computer should display the Windows Desktop, which includes a Start menu, a Taskbar, and Desktop icons.

Navigating Windows Menus

To navigate Windows menus,

1. Place the mouse pointer over the Start button and click to open the Start menu.

 Each mouse action has a different effect on an object. Typically, clicking selects an object, double-clicking opens or runs an object, and right-clicking brings up a context-sensitive menu. Sometimes all you need to do is hover the mouse pointer over an item to initiate an action; doing so normally opens an additional menu or gives you pop-up definitions.

2. In the open Start menu, move the mouse pointer to the Programs item and hover. Doing so opens the Programs submenu. In Windows XP, move the mouse to All Programs.

> The small arrows at the right edge of any menu tell you that submenus are available.

3. In the Programs submenu, move the mouse pointer to the Accessories item and either click or hover to open the Accessories submenu. In Windows XP, move the mouse to All Programs.

4. In the Accessories submenu, place the mouse pointer on Notepad. Click the mouse to open the Notepad program.

5. Close the open Notepad window by clicking the Close (X) button in the upper-right corner of the window. Doing so returns you to the Desktop.

Shutting Down Windows Using a Mouse

To shut down Windows using a mouse,

1. Click the Close button on all open windows. Doing so returns you to the Desktop.

2. To shut down Windows, follow these steps:

   In Windows 98, click the Start button, click Shut Down, and then select Shut Down.

   > Start ➢ Shut Down➢ Shut Down

   In Windows 2000:

   > Start ➢ Shut Down➢ Shut Down

   In Windows XP:

   > Start ➢ Turn Off Computer➢ Turn Off

> Do not turn off your computer until you see a message that says you can safely do so. Normally, an ATX computer turns itself off. If it doesn't, press and hold the power button to turn it off.

Shutting Down Windows Using the Keyboard

To shut down Windows using the keyboard,

1. Press Alt+Tab to cycle between all open programs. Then, press Alt+F4 to close the programs one at a time.

2. Open the Start menu by pressing the Windows logo key or by pressing Ctrl+Esc.

3. Press the Up Arrow key to highlight a menu option on the Start menu. Follow the sequence list in the previous exercise for each of the operating systems to complete the shutdown. If you need to access the buttons in a window, press the Tab key to cycle between them.

Alternatively, you can press Ctrl+Alt+Del. In Windows 98, this action brings up the Close Program window. You can shut down the computer by pressing the Tab key until the Shut Down button is active. In Windows 2000/XP, this action brings up the Windows Security window. From there, you can Tab to the Shut Down or Turn Off button.

Starting a Windows Command-line Session

In Windows 98:

1. Use the following sequence to start a command-line session:

    Start ➤ Programs ➤ MS-DOS Prompt

2. When the DOS window opens, you'll see the command prompt (C:\Windows>) displayed in a window.

In Windows 2000:

1. Use the following sequence to start a command-line session:

    Start ➤ Programs ➤ Accessories ➤ Command Prompt

2. When the Command Line window opens, the prompt appears with the path displayed. The path is made up of directory names and is displayed between the drive letter and the prompt.

In Windows XP:

1. Use the following sequence to start a command-line session:

    Start ➤ All Programs ➤ Accessories ➤ Command Prompt

2. When the Command Line window opens, the prompt appears with the path displayed. The path is made up of directory names and is displayed between the drive letter and the prompt.

Navigating in a Windows Command-line Session

To navigate in a Windows command-line session,

1. Type the command **CD** to change to the root directory.

After entering each command, you need to press Enter for the command to execute.

2. Type **CLS** to clear the screen:

    C:\>**CLS**

3. To display the contents of the root directory, execute the directory command (DIR) by typing the following command:

    C:\>**DIR**

Subdirectories are enclosed in angle brackets (<>).

4. To create a new directory, use the MD command (Make Directory). Type **MD CLTEST** to create a test directory for this exercise:

   C:\>**MD CLTEST**

5. To redisplay the contents of the root directory and see the new directory, type **DIR**:

   C:\>**DIR**

6. To open a directory or subdirectory, type **CD** (Change Directory) followed by a space, and then type the name of the subdirectory. Enter the following to open the CLTEST directory:

   C:\>**CD CLTEST**

7. Now, when you enter the directory command, the files in the CLTEST directory will scroll by. The new directory should only be two entries, one for the parent directory (. .) and the other for the current directory (.):

   C:\Cltest>**DIR**

8. Type the command **CD** to change to the root directory:

   C:\Cltest>**CD**

9. Open the directory that stores the operating system. In Windows 98, the directory is called Windows; in Windows 2000/XP, it is Winnt.

   In Windows 98, type

   C:\>**CD WINDOWS**

   In Windows 2000/XP, type

   C:\>**CD WINNT**

10. To display the contents of the current directory, type **DIR**. Watch as the files scroll by.

11. To obtain help with the DIR command, type **DIR /?**, the pipe symbol (|), and then **MORE** at the prompt:

    C:\Windows>**DIR /? | MORE**

    Read the screen about the DIR command. When you are ready to move to the next screen, press Enter.

12. To pause the DIR command, you use the /P switch. Type **DIR /P** at the prompt:

    C:\Windows>**DIR /P**

After you use the /P switch, press Enter or the spacebar to page down and see the next screen. Continue to press Enter or the spacebar until you complete the action. To stop the action, you can press Ctrl+C.

Exiting a Windows Command-line Session

When the C: prompt is displayed as shown here, type **EXIT** to return to the Windows Desktop:

C:\Windows>**EXIT**

Computers that use DOS for an operating system can be turned off when the command prompt is displayed. However, Windows computers must be returned to the Windows GUI before you can shut them down.

Lab Report 11.1

1. How do you close a window using the mouse?

    _____

    _____

    _____

    _____

2. Which Windows interface allows you to see the Programs or All Programs menu?

    _____

    _____

    _____

    _____

3. What is the shutdown sequence for Windows 98?

_____

_____

_____

_____

4. If you don't have a mouse or the mouse is not working, how can you safely shut down the computer in Windows 98?

_____

_____

_____

_____

_____

Lab 11.2: Customizing the Windows Desktop

Windows permits you to customize the Desktop and give your computer a personality of its own. You can arrange the Desktop icons, create shortcuts, and customize the Start menu.

Upon completion of this lab, you will be able to:

- Arrange the shortcuts on the Desktop
- Create a shortcut on the Desktop
- Change the Start menu

Set Up

For this lab, you will need a working PC with Windows installed. It is best if you can boot into Windows 98, Windows 2000, and Windows XP to notice the differences between the operating systems.

Exercises

In this lab, you will arrange the Desktop icons, create shortcuts on the Desktop, change display properties, and change the Start menu.

Arranging Icons on the Desktop

Icons on the Desktop are generally shortcuts to applications or tools that are frequently used. Some common examples tools are My Computer and the Recycle Bin. Each operating system has its own set of icons that it places on the Desktop by default.

1. Right-click an empty area of the Desktop. A context-sensitive menu will appear.

2. Place the mouse pointer over Arrange Icons to display a submenu that lets you select a method to arrange the Desktop icons.

3. From the submenu, select Auto Arrange to automatically place the Desktop icons into columns. Pull an icon out of line and move it to the bottom of the column. Notice what happens.

> The icons can be arranged by name, type, size, or date. Click on the desired icon to implement your desired arrangement.

4. Right-click in an empty area of the Desktop to bring up the context-sensitive menu. Hover the mouse over Arrange Icons and deselect Auto Arrange from the submenu.

5. Click and drag the icons on the Desktop to different locations on the Desktop.

> The click-and-drag operations require that you click the left mouse button and hold it down while you move the mouse to the desired location. When the mouse is at the new location, release the left mouse button. This technique allows you to move objects inside a window as well as between windows.

6. Right-click the mouse on an empty area of the Desktop to bring up the context-sensitive menu. Click Line Up Icons to make the icons snap to the invisible grid on the Desktop, lining them up.

Creating a Shortcut

Shortcuts are icons that allow you to easily run programs or open folders without needing to manually locate them each time. Double-clicking a shortcut to a file executes it. You can create shortcuts to any object, such as a directory or an application program. In this exercise you will create a shortcut for the Notepad and Solitaire applications and place them on the Desktop.

There are several ways to create shortcuts, and this exercise covers two of them. The best technique is the one that you find easier.

1. Right-click on an empty area of the Desktop. From the context-sensitive menu, select New ≻ Shortcut.

2. In the Create Shortcut window, click Browse. This option will let you find the Notepad executable file. In Windows 98 and Windows XP, you can find Notepad in the `C:\Windows` directory. In Windows 2000, it is in the `C:\Winnt\System32` directory. Use the drop-down menu in the Look In field to navigate to the appropriate directory.

3. Click on the `Notepad.exe` icon to automatically enter its information in the Command Line field. Click Next.

4. In the Select a Title for the Program window, change the name from `Notepad.exe` to just `Notepad`. Click Finish. This step creates an icon on the Desktop in the place where you right-clicked the mouse.

5. Double-click on My Computer.

6. Double-click the icon for drive C:.

    In Windows 98 and Windows XP:

    > Double-click the icon for the `Windows` directory and locate the Solitaire icon (`sol.exe`), using the scroll bars if necessary.

    In Windows 2000:

    > Double-click the icon for the `Winnt` directory and then double-click `System32`. Locate the `sol.exe` file.

7. Click and drag the icon to the Desktop to create a shortcut on the Desktop.

8. Double-click the new Notepad shortcut. The Notepad utility should run. Double-click the Solitaire icon to open Solitaire.

9. Close Notepad and Solitaire.

Customizing the Start Menu

The Start menu is essentially a list of shortcuts used to quickly access frequently used programs. Although it is possible to place shortcuts to all your favorite programs on the Desktop, many people dislike a cluttered Desktop. In addition, each shortcut displayed on the Desktop uses a small amount of memory, and this memory can add up. To free up system memory, some people prefer to place these shortcuts in the Start menu. Before you begin this process, note the location of the files and/or directories for which you want to create Start menu shortcuts. In this lab, you will place Notepad into the Start menu using one method and then place Solitaire into the Start menu using another method.

1. Right-click the Start button and select Open.

2. Locate the Notepad icon on the Desktop. Click and drag the Notepad icon onto the Start menu window.

3. Click and drag the Solitaire icon onto the Start button.

4. Click on the Start button. Notice the two new icons.

Lab Report 11.2

1. What occurs when you right-click an open area of the Desktop?

_____

_____

_____

_____

2. What is the Start menu?

_____

_____

_____

_____

3. What is the function of a shortcut?

_____

_____

_____

_____

4. How do you add a program to the Start menu?

_____

_____

_____

_____

Lab 11.3: Using Files and Folders

When you use a computer, you are using files and folders. The ability to find and manipulate files or folders efficiently is an essential skill.

Upon completion of this lab, you will be able to:

- Create a folder
- Copy a file or folder within the same drive
- Copy a file or folder between different drives
- Use Find or Search to locate a file or folder

Set Up

For this lab, you will need a working PC with either Windows98, Windows 2000, or Windows XP installed and a blank floppy disk for drive A:.

Exercises

In this lab, you will create a folder, copy a file or folder, delete a file or folder, and use Find to locate a file or folder. Often, files need to be moved or copied from one folder to another or from one drive to another. This lab shows one method of copying files and creating folders.

Creating a Folder

The ability to create new folders is essential to keep your files organized properly.

1. Double-click the My Computer icon to open the My Computer window. In Windows XP, My Computer is found in the Start menu.
2. Double-click the Drive C: icon and then double-click the My Documents icon.

3. Use this sequence to create a new folder:

    File ➢ New ➢ Folder

4. When the new folder appears in the window, type a folder name in place of New Folder. In this case, type the name **Test1** and press Enter.

5. Right-click in an empty area of the C: drive window. From the context-sensitive menu, choose

    New ➢ Folder

6. When the new folder appears, type **Test2** and press Enter.

7. Double-click the Test1 folder. When the folder opens, it should be empty. Leave this window open; you will use it in the next exercise.

Copying a File within the Same Drive

The procedure for copying a file and a folder are identical. The Copy and Cut commands are identical *except* that the Cut command deletes the original file after the file has been moved, or *pasted*, to its destination. In both cases, the file is copied to the Windows Clipboard. The Clipboard is a temporary area in memory that holds information being copied or cut.

1. In the Test1 folder, right-click on a blank area of the window.

 When you are experimenting with new commands, be safe and don't use valuable files. Create a test file.

2. From the context menu, select

    New ➢ Text Document

3. When the new text file appears in the Test1 window, enter a filename in place of New Text Document. In this case, type the name **Doc1** and press Enter.

4. Right-click the Doc1 file and select Copy from the context-sensitive menu.

5. Click on the Up button in the standard button bar to return to My Documents. Double-click on the Test2 folder.

6. Right-click in a blank area of the Test2 window and select Paste. The Doc1 file should appear. Leave this window open; you will use it in the next exercise.

Copying a File or Folder between Two Drives

The procedures for copying files and folders are identical.

1. Place a blank formatted floppy disk into drive A:.

2. Right-click the Doc1 file and select Copy from the context-sensitive menu.

3. Click on the Up button twice in the standard button bar to return to My Computer. Double-click on the A: drive.

4. Right-click a blank area in the drive A: window and select Paste.

5. You should observe the file being copied. This is a small file, so the copy time is only a few seconds.

6. Remove the floppy disk.

Deleting and Restoring a File or Folder

The procedures for deleting files and folders are identical. You cannot restore files or folders that have been deleted from drive A:.

1. Double-click the My Computer icon to open the My Computer window. In Windows XP, My Computer is located in the Start menu.

2. In the My Computer window, double-click drive C:.

3. Right-click on the folder Test1. From the context menu, select Delete.

4. In the Confirm Folder Delete window, click Yes.

5. Restoring the folder is quick and easy if you have not performed any other editing options since it was deleted. (Windows allows you to undo your last editing option.) To restore the file, choose Edit ➢ Undo Delete. The folder should reappear in the drive C: window.

6. Delete the folder again. See step 3 for help.

7. A second method of restoring a deleted file involves the Recycle Bin. Double-click the Recycle Bin icon on the Desktop.

8. In the Recycle Bin window, locate and right-click the Test1 folder. Select Restore from the menu. The Test1 folder and its contents are placed back in the original location. Verify this by opening the drive C: window and locating the Test1 folder.

Using the *Find* Command to Locate a File or Folder

To find a file or folder,

1. Use the following:

   In Windows 98:

       Start ➢ Find ➢ Files or Folders

   In Windows 2000:

       Start ➢ Search ➢ For Files or Folders

   In Windows XP:

       Start ➢ Search ➢ All Files or Folders

2. You have many options when using Find. For a basic search, select the target in the Look In box. Select drive C:.

3. Type the name of the file or folder you want to locate in the box. If you know only part of the name, you can use an asterisk to represent any unknown characters. In Windows XP, it is not necessary to use the *, because XP automatically searches for all or part of a name.

For instance, type **read*** in the search criteria box to locate any files or folders that begin with the characters *read* followed by any other characters. Click Find Now.

4. A list of all the files beginning with the characters *read* is displayed in the Find window along with each file's location, size, type, and date of last modification. The vertical scroll bar permits you to view files that are not visible in the window. The horizontal scroll bar permits you to view more information about the files displayed in the window.

5. To execute a file from the Find window, double-click the filename.

Lab Report 11.3

1. What is the Clipboard?

_____

_____

_____

_____

2. When do you use cut and paste? When do you use copy and paste?

_____

_____

_____

_____

3. How do you open the Recycle Bin?

_____

_____

_____

_____

4. What is the purpose of the asterisk in the Find dialog box?

_____

_____

_____

_____

Lab 11.4: Installing and Launching Applications

There are several ways to install an application in a Windows system. Most users have one method they use to install applications. However, sometimes an attempt to install an application fails, and the solution is to attempt the installation by a different method.

Upon completion of this lab, you will be able to:

- Install an application in a Windows system
- Launch an application in a Windows system

Set Up

For this lab, you will need:

- A working PC with Windows installed
- The application software you want to install

Exercises

In this lab, you will use several methods to install and launch programs in Windows. Installations are usually easier if you close all application programs before you begin the installation process.

Installing a Program in Windows

To install a program under Windows, follow the instructions supplied with the software. The instructions are often found in a Readme file on the software disk or in an instruction manual accompanying the software. Use one of the following procedures to install application software.

Sometimes, a particular piece of software will install when one procedure is used, but it will not install when a different procedure is used.

Using Autorun to Install Applications

If the software is supplied on a CD-ROM, insert the CD-ROM into the CD-ROM drive. Most CD-ROMs automatically run and display an installation screen. You should be able to select Install from a displayed menu. Follow any on-screen instructions that are provided.

Using Add/Remove Programs to Install Applications

Windows provides an Add/Remove Programs utility to help you manage the installed software on a PC. This utility is found in Control Panel. Add/Remove Programs helps you to install, upgrade, and remove software:

1. In Control Panel, double-click Add/Remove Programs and click Install.

2. Insert the CD-ROM or disk containing the software you want to install. When the drive activity light goes out, click Next.

3. Follow the on-screen instructions provided.

Using Run to Install Applications

Another way to begin the installation process is via the Run command. This method requires that you know or be able to browse for the path of the installation or setup command:

1. Choose Start ➢ Run from the Windows Desktop.

2. Put the CD from this book into the CD-ROM.

3. In the Open text box, enter the pathname and filename of the installation file. For example, enter the following to run the `clickme.exe` program located in the root directory of the D: drive or the drive letter of the CD-ROM:

   D:\clickme.exe

4. Click OK, and then follow any on-screen instructions provided.

Using My Computer to Install Applications

You can also install files directly from an executable file residing in a directory (My Computer, for instance):

1. In the My Computer window, double-click the drive icon of the drive containing the program you want to install.

2. Look for files that may install the software (such as `install.exe` or `setup.exe`).

3. Double-click on the setup utility icon to execute the installation program. Follow any on-screen instructions provided.

Launching an Application Program in a Windows System

Once you have a program installed, you need to launch it in order to use it. There are four methods of launching a program under Windows:

- Double-click its icon on the Desktop.
- Double-click the program in Windows Explorer.
- Select the program in the Start menu.
- Enter the pathname and filename in the Run dialog box.

  For this lab, you will use these methods to launch the Notepad program.

Launching a Program Using My Computer

Users frequently place shortcuts to their favorite programs on the Desktop. To execute a program using its shortcut, double-click the program's shortcut icon. If the program does not have a shortcut on the Desktop, you must locate the program before you launch it:

1. Open the My Computer window.

2. Double-click the drive containing the program to be launched. The Windows directory should be on drive C:, so double-click the drive C: icon.

3. Double-click the folder containing the program to be launched. In some cases, you may need to open more than one folder (or *drill down*) to reach the desired file, if it is several layers deep. For example, in Windows 98 and Windows XP, the Notepad application is in the Windows folder. In Windows 2000, Notepad can be found in the System32 folder.

4. Locate the program in its folder, using the scroll bars, if necessary, to view all the files. Double-click the Notepad file to launch Notepad. You may also right-click the program and select Open from the pop-up menu; however, most users find it easier to double-click.

5. Close the Notepad utility. Always be sure to look at your Taskbar (the bar at the bottom of your Desktop) to make sure none of the windows or programs is minimized. Click any minimized program to maximize it so you can close it properly. Remember that even when a program or window is minimized, it is still using system resources!

Launching a Program from the Start Menu

Not all programs have entries on the Start menu. Most new programs add entries at the time of installation. You can manually add a shortcut for any program that didn't automatically add one to the Start menu.

1. Choose Start ➢ Programs. In Windows XP, select Start ➢ All Programs.

2. An icon for the program you want to launch may be visible on the Start menu, or an icon may be in one of the folders displayed in the Start menu. If you select a folder that has an arrow, its contents are displayed. In this case, the Notepad utility is in the Accessories folder. Select the Accessories folder and click Notepad to launch the application.

3. Close Notepad.

Launching a Program Using the Run Command

This method is generally used only when you know the path and full MS-DOS name of the file to be executed. For example, you can use `C:\Windows\Notepad.exe` as your path and filename. If you do not know the path for the program, you can browse and find it.

1. Choose Start ➢ Run.

2. In the Open text box, type the path and filename of the program you want to launch, or browse to the directory containing the file.

    In Windows 98, type

    `C:\WINDOWS\NOTEPAD.EXE`

    Click OK.

    In Windows 2000/XP, type

    `C:\WINNT\SYSTEM32\NOTEPAD.EXE`

    Click OK.

3. Close all of the open windows.

Lab Report 11.4

1. If you purchase application software that has no book of installation instructions, where will you usually find such instructions?

    _____

    _____

    _____

    _____

2. Which application-launching procedure has the fewest steps?

    _____

    _____

    _____

    _____

3. How do you close an open application that has been minimized?

_____

_____

_____

_____

4. Can all applications be installed by each of the procedures in this lab?

_____

_____

_____

_____

Answers to Lab Reports

Lab Report 11.1

1. To use a mouse to close a window, click the close button in the upper-right corner of the screen.
2. The Start menu.
3. Start ➤ Shut Down ➤ Shut Down ➤ OK.
4. Press Alt+Tab to cycle between all open programs. Press Alt+F4 to close all open programs one at a time. Press the Windows logo key to open the Start menu. Press U to activate the Shutdown icon. Press S to select the Shutdown option, and then press Enter.

Lab Report 11.2

1. A context-sensitive menu will open.
2. The main menu in the Windows interface.
3. To open a file, folder, or program more quickly.
4. Open the Start menu by right-clicking on it and selecting Open, and then drag the icons of the desired programs into the Start menu window.

Lab Report 11.3

1. Memory space used to hold information that is being copied or cut.
2. You cut and paste when you want to remove information from its location and place it in another location. You copy and paste when you want the information to remain in its present location and you also want a second copy of the information.
3. There are two options: Right-click the Recycle Bin icon and select Open from the menu, or double-click the Recycle Bin icon.
4. The asterisk is a wildcard you can use to represent any number of unknown letters.

Lab Report 11.4

1. In the Readme file on the installation disk.
2. Autorun has the fewest steps.
3. Click the minimized program to maximize it. Then close the program or right-click the Taskbar item and select Close from the menu.
4. No. Sometimes a program will not install with a particular method but will install with another method.

Chapter 12

Major OS Architectures

LABS YOU WILL PERFORM IN THIS CHAPTER:

✓ Lab 12.1: Creating an Emergency Repair Disk

✓ Lab 12.2: Creating an Automated System Recovery Disk

One of the worst disasters that can happen to your system is for your system configuration information to become corrupted or lost. We are used to backing up our data files, but we frequently overlook the system configuration information. Trying to duplicate the configuration is a very time consuming task, so Microsoft has built in a way to copy the key configuration information. In Windows 2000 we use the Emergency Repair Disk, and in Windows XP we use an updated version called Automated System Recovery Disk.

 For more information, see Chapter 13 of David Groth's *A+ Complete Study Guide* (Sybex, 2003).

Lab 12.1: Creating an Emergency Repair Disk

One of the many tools used to preserve the system configuration in Windows NT and Windows 2000 is the Emergency Repair Disk (ERD). The ERD contains key system configuration data that is used during the emergency repair process to restore the system to an operating state. You must remember that the ERD is not a bootable disk. Once the emergency repair process starts, you are prompted to insert the ERD to recover the key sections of the Registry.

It is recommended that you create an ERD every time you update the system configuration. Doing so is part of the backup process. This exercise will walk you through the process to create the ERD.

Upon completion of this lab, you will be able to:

- Create an Emergency Repair Disk

Set Up

For this lab, you will need a computer running Windows 2000 and a blank disk labeled *Emergency Repair Disk*.

Exercise

To create an Emergency Repair Disk,

1. Start the Windows 2000 Backup program:

    Start ➤ Programs ➤ Accessories ➤ System Tools ➤ Backup

2. On the Welcome tab, click the Emergency Repair Disk button.

3. In the Emergency Repair Disk window, select the option Also Backup the Registry to the Repair Directory. This step creates or updates the Registry files stored in the Repair directory. You can use these files if the ERD becomes damaged.

4. Label a floppy disk **Emergency Repair Disk** and insert it into the floppy drive. Click Next to continue.

5. When the system has finished writing the files onto the disk, click OK to finish.

6. Close the Backup utility.

Lab Report 12.1

1. What information is stored on the ERD?

    _____

    _____

    _____

    _____

2. How do you access the utility used to create the ERD?

    _____

    _____

    _____

    _____

3. Where is the alternate location for the information stored on the ERD?

    _____

    _____

    _____

    _____

4. When should you update the ERD?

_____

_____

_____

_____

Lab 12.2: Creating an Automated System Recovery Disk

Windows 2000 uses an ERD as part of a system to recover if the system's configuration becomes corrupted or the system crashes. Windows XP enhances this process in the Automated System Recovery (ASR). ASR is an integrated part of backups. First, the system creates a backup of the system partition; then it creates a recovery disk that is used to restore the system to a fully functional state.

We all know that creating backups is a vital part of any system management plan. Windows XP makes it easy to back up not only data but also the system configuration information. This process is known as Automated System Recovery. It should be part of a regular backup plan.

Upon completion of this lab, you will be able to:

- Create an Automated System Recovery disk

Set Up

For this lab, you will need a computer running Windows XP and a floppy disk labeled *Automated System Recovery Disk*.

Exercise

To create an automated system recovery disk,

1. Open the Backup utility:

    Start ➤ All Programs ➤ Accessories ➤ System Tools ➤ Backup

2. In the initial window, click the Advanced Mode link to open the Welcome to the Backup Utility Advanced Mode screen.

NOTE   Initially the Backup utility will want to open in Wizard mode. You need to deselect Wizard mode, close Backup and reopen the Backup utility

3. Click the Automated System Recovery Wizard button.

4. In the Welcome to the Automated System Recovery Preparation Wizard window, click Next to continue.

5. In the Backup Destination window, verify that the file backup.bkf will be created on the A: drive.

6. Label a floppy disk **Automated System Recovery Disk** and insert it into the floppy drive.

7. Click Next to continue to the last window. Review the information presented on the screen. Click Finish to write the file to the disk.

Lab Report 12.2

1. What information is stored on the ASR disk?

_____

_____

_____

_____

2. How do you access the ASR Wizard?

_____

_____

_____

_____

3. What file is created by default on the ASR disk?

    _____

    _____

    _____

    _____

4. When should you create or update the ASR disk?

    _____

    _____

    _____

    _____

Answers to Lab Reports

Lab Report 12.1

1. The ERD contains the parts of the Registry that include the system configuration data.
2. You create the ERD through the Backup utility.
3. The information on the ERD is also stored in the Repair directory.
4. You should update the ERD every time a system configuration change is made.

Lab Report 12.2

1. The ASR disk contains the system configuration information.
2. The wizard used to create or update the disk used for ASR is found in the Backup utility.
3. The default name of the file is `backup.bkf`.
4. You should back up the system configuration each time you successfully update it. Doing so updates the disk used by the ASR.

Chapter 13

Installing and Upgrading Your OS

LABS YOU WILL PERFORM IN THIS CHAPTER:

✓ Lab 13.1: Using *FDISK* and *FORMAT*

✓ Lab 13.2: Installing Windows 98

✓ Lab 13.3: Installing Windows 2000 Professional

✓ Lab 13.4: Installing Windows XP

Before any computer can be used, an operating system needs to be installed. And before the operating system can be installed, the hard drive needs to be prepared for use. If you decide to build your own computer or upgrade the hard drive, you will have to prepare the hard drive for use and then install the operating system. If you purchase a ready-to-use computer, you may want to reinstall the operating system for the experience you will gain. You will probably upgrade an operating system sometime in the life of the computer, so it is always a good idea to understand the installation process.

This chapter covers the FDISK and FORMAT utilities that allow you to prepare a hard drive for use. We will discuss the steps necessary to install Windows 98, Windows 2000, and Windows XP. To become proficient at installation, you may want to consider obtaining a separate hard drive that can be FDISKed and formatted, and on which you can install all the operating systems covered in this chapter.

I recommend getting a hard drive and creating three separate partitions, one for each of the operating systems we will cover. In subsequent chapters you will be able to multiboot your system; this will let you complete all the labs. If you are going to multiboot your system, you need to install Windows 98 first, followed by Windows 2000, and finally Windows XP. When you boot, you will be able to select the operating system from a menu. To change to one of the other operating systems, reboot and select the new operating system from the same menu.

For more information, see Chapter 14 of David Groth's *A+ Complete Study Guide* (Sybex, 2003).

Lab 13.1: Using *FDISK* and *FORMAT*

Before you can use a hard drive to install an operating system or any other software, you must prepare it and make it ready. This process is called partitioning and formatting. *Partitioning* is the process of creating space on the hard drive for use as either partitions or volumes. *Formatting* is the process of placing a filesystem into the partition so that the space is usable. This lab covers using the FDISK utility with the Windows 98 operating system. This is a common tool to help you prepare for the installation. Windows 2000/XP have their own version of FDISK included in the installation process.

There are two types of partitions, primary and extended. *Primary partitions* are the more common of the two types. The user sees each partition as a drive letter, such as C:. An *extended partition* can be subdivided into multiple logical drives. A separate drive letter represents each of the logical drives.

You can use the FDISK utility to create partitions on the hard drive. You have several options as to how the drive is partitioned:

- Create one large partition that includes all available space on the hard drive.

- Break up the hard drive into smaller pieces to create an optimized drive that uses smaller cluster sizes.

- Split the drive into functional units, such as a partition for the operating system, another for applications, and another for data. This option makes backups easier.

If you already have a partially partitioned hard drive, you can use FDISK to create additional partitions on the remaining available space. You can also use FDISK at any time to see what partitions exist on the hard drive.

After you have partitioned the hard drive into usable sections, you need to format it. This lab will cover the FORMAT utility that is included on the Windows 98 boot disk. Again, Windows 2000/XP have their own FORMAT utilities included in the install program, so we will not cover them separately.

Upon completion of this lab, you will be able to:

- Partition a hard drive

- Format a partition

Set Up

For this lab, you will need a Windows 98 boot disk with the FDISK utility and a hard drive that can be partitioned.

 If you are using a hard drive that has existing partitions and you remove a partition, all the information in the partition will be lost.

Exercises

In this exercise you will use the FDISK and FORMAT utilities.

Using *FDISK*

To use the FDISK utility,

1. Insert the Windows 98 boot disk with the FDISK utility into the floppy drive and start the computer.

2. At the command prompt, type **FDISK**.

3. FDISK does a check of your hard drive. If the hard drive is bigger than 512MB, FDISK asks if you want to enable large-disk support. It gives you a default response of Y for Yes. Press Enter to enable large-disk support.

4. FDISK presents a menu with five options if you have multiple drives installed. Or, if you only have one drive, the Change Current Fixed Disk Drive option does not appear. See Figure 13.1.

FIGURE 13.1   FDISK menu

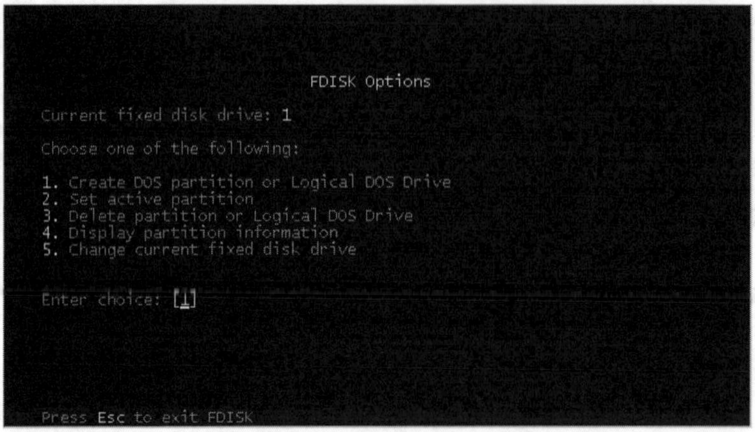

```
                         FDISK Options
Current fixed disk drive: 1

Choose one of the following:

    1. Create DOS partition or Logical DOS Drive
    2. Set active partition
    3. Delete partition or Logical DOS Drive
    4. Display partition information
    5. Change current fixed disk drive


Enter choice: [1]



Press Esc to exit FDISK
```

5. To view what partitions, if any, already exist on the hard drive, select option 4 from the menu by typing **4** in the Enter Choice field. Press Enter.

6. You will see all existing partitions and available hard-drive space in the Display Partition Information screen. If you have extended partitions, you can choose to view the extended partition information. Make a note of any existing partition information:

    Status:

    _____

    _____

    Type of partition:

    _____

    _____

7. Press the Esc key to return to the main screen.

8. If the disk has existing partitions, you need to delete them. If the drive is new, skip to step 12. To delete existing partitions, type **3** in the Enter Choice field and then press Enter.

9. From the Delete Primary DOS Partition or Logical DOS Drive screen, select the type of partition recorded in step 6.

10. From the Delete Partition Screen, select the partition to be deleted and then press Enter.

11. Repeat steps 9 and 10 until all partitions have been deleted.

12. Press Esc until you are returned to the FDISK Options screen.

13. You will now create a new partition. Enter **1** in the Enter Choice field and press Enter.

14. In the Create Partition or Logical Drive screen, select option 1 to create a primary DOS partition.

15. FDISK asks if you want to use the maximum space available to create the new disk. You will create a 3GB partition for the C: drive, which is adequate for most operating systems. The rest of the hard drive can then be used for your applications and data. If your hard drive is smaller than 4GB, then use all of the available space. Press N in the Use Maximum Space Available field. FDISK will prompt you for the amount of drive space you want to allocate for the drive, in megabytes. Type **3000** to create the 3GB drive. Press Enter to complete the action.

16. Press Esc until you are back at the FDISK Options screen.

17. Select option 2 to set the active partition. In the Set Active Partition Screen, select partition 1 and press Enter.

18. Press Esc until you are asked to reboot the computer for the changes to take effect.

Using *FORMAT*

To use the FORMAT utility,

1. After the computer restarts from the previous exercise, you need to format the newly created partition. At the command prompt, type **FORMAT C: /s**.

You must be at the A: prompt. The C: prompt should not be available.

2. A warning appears, which states that all information will be lost if you continue. Type **Y** to confirm the action.

3. FORMAT will format the C: drive with FAT32.

Lab Report 13.1

1. What is the difference between the FDISK and FORMAT commands?

_____

_____

_____

_____

2. What types of partitions does FDISK recognize?

_____

_____

_____

_____

3. What is an extended partition?

_____

_____

_____

_____

4. How do you tell the computer which drive to boot from?

_____

_____

_____

_____

Lab 13.2: Installing Windows 98

With Windows 98, Microsoft raised the level of expectation in an operating system by adding a number of improvements to previous Windows OSs. Windows 98 brought end users a better user interface, improved Plug and Play (PnP), and support for new devices like DVD, FireWire, and modems. Windows 98 can support both FAT16 and FAT32 partitions. Networking added support for Virtual Private Networks (VPNs) and Layer 2 Tunneling Protocol (L2TP). Internet capability improved with tighter integration between Internet Explorer and Windows Explorer.

The Internet Connection Wizard integrated dial-up networking, making it simpler to connect to the Internet. The use of new wizards made all tasks easier to complete, ranging from setting up devices to installing the operating system.

Windows 98's was the first user-friendly installation that resulted in a complete installation. This section will cover the installation by having you follow the Installation Wizard to complete the entire configuration. The key to following the wizard is to read the screens and follow the recommendations made by the computer.

The minimum hardware requirements for installing Windows 98 are as follows:

Processor	486–66MHz
RAM	16MB
Disk Space	110MB

Upon completion of this lab, you will be able to install Windows 98.

Set Up

For this lab, you will need a computer that meets the hardware requirements for installing Windows 98 and a Windows 98 Installation CD.

Exercise

You will use the hard drive you partitioned and formatted in the previous lab.

1. Set the CMOS boot sequence to seek the CD-ROM drive first.

2. Place the Windows 98 installation CD in the CD-ROM drive and boot the computer.

3. If you are prompted during the POST sequence, select Boot from CD-ROM.

4. When you are prompted, select Start Windows 98 Setup from CD-ROM.

5. Setup performs a number of routine checks. The first is ScanDisk. Press Enter to allow the system to verify the integrity of the hard drive.

6. When all the files have been copied to the hard drive and you are instructed to reboot the computer, choose Boot to the Hard Drive.

7. Set the CMOS to seek drive A: first, and reboot the computer.

8. The first screen that appears is the License Agreement window. Click I Accept the Agreement and click Next.

9. The Product Key window appears. Enter the 25-digit product key that can be found on the back of the CD container. Click Next to continue.

10. In the next window, select the directory where Windows 98 is to be installed. Click on the C:\WINDOWS option and then click Next.

11. The Setup utility creates the directory, looks for any installed components, and verifies drive space. The next screen prompts you for the type of installation. For this install, click Typical and then click Next.

12. The setup wizard asks for the user information. Type in your name and your company's name. It is mandatory to enter something in the Name field; once you do, the Next button is available. Click Next.

13. The next window asks which Windows Components you want to install. Select Install the Most Common Components and click Next.

14. Setup asks for your location. Select the appropriate location from the list and click Next.

15. Setup now wants to create a startup disk. Place a blank floppy into the floppy drive and click Next.

16. Windows begins to install the necessary components to your hard drive. Once it is finished, the system will restart and Windows 98 will attempt to detect any Plug-and-Play devices. You should have the files on hand to complete the installation of the device drivers. Once the device drivers have been installed, you computer is ready for you to use.

Lab Report 13.2

1. What filesystems are supported by Windows 98?

_____

_____

_____

_____

2. What is the minimum processor for Windows 98?

_____

_____

_____

_____

3. What are two features introduced with Windows 98?

_____

_____

_____

_____

Lab 13.3: Installing Windows 2000 Professional

Windows 2000 is based on the Windows NT technologies. Although the user interface is very similar to that of Windows 98, the Windows 2000 architecture is significantly different. Windows 2000 was designed to take the best features from both families of operating systems that Microsoft supports. The reliability, stability, and security come from the Windows NT family, and the user interface, PnP support, and new hardware support come from the Windows 98 side. Windows 2000 was released in four flavors: Professional, Server, Advanced Server, and Data Center. Each variation targeted specific needs of the targeted users, everyone from home users to large corporate networks. In this lab, you will begin by installing Windows 2000 Professional to learn how the operating system works.

The minimum hardware requirements for installing Windows 2000 are as follows:

Processor	Pentium 133
RAM	64MB
Disk Space	650MB

Upon completion of this lab, you will be able to:

- Create Windows 2000 setup boot disks
- Install Windows 2000 Professional

Set Up

For this lab, you will need:

- A computer that meets the hardware requirements for installing Windows 2000 Professional
- A Windows 2000 Installation CD

- Four floppies for the first exercise
- A set of Windows 2000 setup disks for the first exercise (you can make them on any Windows computer)

Exercises

This lab will cover the installation process for Windows 2000. It will also describe the steps necessary if your computer will not boot from the CD-ROM. The first exercise shows you how to create the four Windows 2000 boot disks you use to start the installation. If your computer can boot from the CD-ROM, then you can boot the computer using the CD and begin at step 5.

Installing Windows 2000 on a Computer That Does Not Have a Bootable CD-ROM Drive

To install Windows 2000 on a computer that does not have a bootable CD-ROM drive,

1. Start Windows 98, which you installed in the previous lab. Place the Windows 2000 CD in the CD-ROM drive.

2. If the Windows 2000 CD opens and asks if you would like to upgrade to Windows 2000, click No and then return to the Desktop.

3. Place a floppy disk in the floppy drive and type the following command:

   `D:\BOOTDISK\MAKEBOOT.EXE A:`

   In this example, D: is the CD-ROM drive letter.

4. Take the set of four Windows 2000 setup disks and the Windows 2000 installation CD to the computer that needs an operating system, and boot to the bootable setup disk.

5. When the Windows Setup screen opens, you need to verify that the source of the distribution files is correct. Make sure that it is reading from the CD-ROM and is pointed to the I386 directory. Press Enter to continue.

6. The setup routine copies files from the CD to your hard drive. You may see a warning about SMARTDRV if you are not using it. When the files have been copied, the computer will restart.

 You may want to stop the installation and run SMARTDRV. It will save you time.

7. When the computer restarts, the Windows 2000 Setup dialog box opens. Press Enter to continue the installation. You also have the option of pressing R to repair an existing installation or F3 to exit.

8. When the Windows 2000 License agreement screen appears, press F8 to accept the license. If you do not accept the license, the installation will halt.

9. The next screens determine which partition and filesystem you want to use. Verify that the C: drive has at least 1GB of free space and then select it. If it does not have at least 1GB free, delete the partition and re-create it with at least 1GB free. Choose to leave the format on the drive using the FAT32 filesystem. The last question asks what directory to use for the installation; leave it as the `WINNT` directory.

10. After the Windows formatting and configuration are complete, reboot the computer by pressing Enter.

11. When the computer boots to Windows 2000, the OS takes control and begins detecting and installing devices. The first dialog box asks for the regional settings. Select the appropriate settings for your region and preferences. Click Next.

12. The next dialog box asks you to enter your name and organization name. You must enter something in the Name field. Type your first name in the Name field. If you desire, you can enter an organization name. Click Next.

13. The Product Key dialog box is next. You must enter the product key found on the yellow sticker on the case for the CD. Click Next.

14. The Computer Name and Administrator Password Dialog box opens. The computer name is based on the name you entered in step 12, with some random characters added to the end. You can type a new computer name, if you wish. The dialog box also asks for the password for the administrator account. You need to type it twice for verification. Click Next.

15. The Date and Time Setting dialog box appears next. Here you can verify that the correct date and time are entered into the computer. This information is gathered from the CMOS. Click Next.

16. Next are the Network Settings. You have two choices: Typical and Custom. You will use the Typical settings for this lab. This option installs the Client for Microsoft Networks and TCP/IP using DHCP for automatic configuration. Click Next.

17. Tell the computer if it is a member of a domain or a workgroup. For this lab, install the computer as a member of a workgroup. Click Next to continue.

18. The computer finalizes the installation. When it is done, reboot the computer. Congratulations; you have installed Windows 2000.

Installing Windows 2000 on a Computer That Has an Operating System Installed

To install Windows 2000 on a computer that has an operating system installed,

1. Boot to your current operating system and insert the Windows 2000 CD into the CD-ROM drive.

2. If the Windows 2000 CD opens, click Install Windows 2000. Otherwise, go to step 4.

3. If you are asked if you would like to upgrade your computer to Windows 2000, click No and complete the installation. Follow the on-screen prompts.

4. If the Windows 2000 CD is not automatically detected, start Setup from the Run command by using this sequence:

    Start ➢ Run

5. In the Run dialog box, enter the following command:

    D:\I386\WINNT32.EXE

    D: is the drive letter of the CD-ROM drive.

6. If you are asked if you would like to upgrade your computer to Windows 2000, click No and then complete the installation. Follow the on-screen prompts listed in the previous exercise.

Lab Report 13.3

1. What filesystems are supported by Windows 2000?

    _____

    _____

    _____

    _____

2. What is the minimum amount of free space required to complete the installation?

    _____

    _____

    _____

    _____

3. Which command allows you to create the four Windows 2000 boot disks?

_____

_____

_____

_____

4. What are the different products for Windows 2000?

_____

_____

_____

_____

Lab 13.4: Installing Windows XP

Windows XP comes in two variations, Home and Professional. Windows XP Home is designed to work as a stand-alone unit. It is optimized for the home environment where the needs for network security are not as great. Windows XP Professional is geared toward use in the corporate environment where interconnectivity with other systems is required. Windows XP Professional is designed to interoperate with Windows Servers that are running Active Directory.

This lab will cover the installation of Windows XP Professional. If you have the Windows XP Home edition, the steps are similar, but several steps are not required.

The minimum hardware requirements for installing Windows XP are:

Processor	Pentium 233MHz
RAM	64MB
Disk Space	1.5GB

Upon completion of this lab, you will be able to:

- Install Windows XP Professional
- Activate Windows XP

Set Up

For this lab, you will need a computer that meets the hardware requirements for installing Windows XP and the XP Installation CD.

Exercises

With Windows XP, the first choice you need to make is which edition to install. Then you need to choose whether to upgrade an existing operating system or perform a clean (new) installation. You will perform an upgrade when you want to preserve settings from the previous version of Windows. These setting include user options, custom settings, and applications. You will perform a clean installation when you do not have an existing operating system installed or you want to dual-boot the computer with two different operating systems. You will also perform a clean installation when you are using an operating system that is not compatible with performing an upgrade. This lab will cover the steps needed to perform a clean installation on a computer with an existing operating system installed.

Installing Windows XP

To install Windows XP,

1. Turn on the computer and log in. Place the Windows XP Professional CD into the CD-ROM drive.

 You may have to change the CMOS settings to allow you to boot from the CD-ROM.

2. From the Welcome to Microsoft Windows XP screen, click Install Windows XP to begin the installation process.

3. In the Welcome to Windows Setup window, select New Installation from the Installation Type drop-down menu and click Next.

4. In the License Agreement window, select the I Accept This Agreement option and click Next. If you do not accept the license, the installation will halt.

5. In the Your Product Key window, enter the product key from the yellow sticker on the case of the CD. Click Next.

6. The next window gives you the opportunity to choose advanced and accessibility options and to select the primary language and region. The advanced options allow you to specify source and destination folders and indicate whether you want to choose the install drive letter and partition during the setup process. The accessibility options let you install the Microsoft Magnifier and the Microsoft Narrator. Once you have selected the options and language, click Next to continue.

7. In the Get Updated Setup Files window, you have the chance to use the Dynamic Update to get the latest setup files from Microsoft via the Internet. If you do not have a connection to the Internet, select No, skip this step, and continue installing Windows. If you have a connection to the Internet, you can select Yes to download the updated setup files. If you select this option, your system will collect some information about your computer and then contact the Microsoft website and download all pertinent updated files. Once the update is completed, the system will finish this portion of the setup and then reboot the computer. After the reboot, you will again see the Welcome to Windows Setup screen; press Enter to continue the installation.

8. The partitioning screen gives you a chance to partition your hard drive. You can select the partition for the installation. Select the C: drive and press Enter to continue.

9. If you are installing to a partition that is using FAT, the setup routine gives you the option of converting the installation partition to NTFS. For this lab, ignore the obvious advantages of NTFS and leave the format as FAT.

10. Once the formatting is complete, the setup routine copies files to the hard drive. This process takes several minutes. Then the computer will reboot and start the GUI installation.

11. The first question asks you for the regional and language options. Select the appropriate options for your region and language. Click Next to continue.

12. The next screen asks you to personalize the computer. Enter your name and the name of your organization. An entry in the Name field is required; the organization name is optional. Click Next.

13. You now need to enter the computer name and the password for the administrator account. The name is a byproduct of your name and some randomly generated characters. You can simplify the name by typing an appropriate name. The administrator's password should be unique. You need to type it twice and then click Next to continue.

14. The Date and Time screen has you verify the computer time and date. Click Next.

15. The next step starts to install networking on your computer. You are asked whether you want to install the typical settings or custom settings. Select Typical Settings to install TCP/IP with DHCP enabled. Click Next.

16. The next screen asks if the computer will belong to a workgroup or a computer domain. Select Workgroup and then click Next. The computer will finish copying files and then reboot.

17. In the Welcome to Microsoft Windows screen, click Next.

18. In the next screen, select whether the computer will connect to the Internet directly or through a network. Click Next.

19. The next screen asks if you are ready to register. Select your answer and then click Next. If you selected Yes, fill out the registration fields and then click Next.

20. Fill in the names of the people who will use the computer. Doing so creates user accounts for all of these users. Click Next.

21. Finally, you have completed the installation. Click Finish, and you can begin to use Windows XP.

Activating Windows XP

To activate Windows XP,

1. When Windows XP starts, you are prompted to activate it.

You need to activate Windows XP within 30 days or it will stop working. Although activation seems to be an invasion, it is an attempt to prevent software piracy. You can activate it either over the Internet or by phone. Activation records a unique hardware profile. If you update more than three major components, you will have to reactivate Windows XP.

2. In the Let's Activate Windows window, select the method for activation that is most appropriate for your situation and click Next.

3. If you selected the Internet, the computer gathers some information about your machine and passes it to Microsoft secure server, where it is stored it in a database. You are then automatically given the confirmation code. This process should take only a few seconds to complete. No personal information is collected in this process.

   If you chose to activate over the phone, call the toll-free number on the screen. The customer service representative will ask for the installation ID on the same screen and give you a confirmation code that you need to enter. Once it's entered, the process is complete.

Product registration is an optional process. It is not the same as product activation, which is mandatory. Product registration asks for some personal information.

Lab Report 13.4

1. Windows XP supports which filesystems?

_____

_____

_____

_____

2. What accessibility options can be installed during the setup?

_____

_____

_____

_____

3. Why do you need to activate Windows XP?

_____

_____

_____

_____

4. What information is collected by the activation process?

_____

_____

_____

_____

Answers to Lab Reports

Lab Report 13.1

1. FDISK creates the space for the partition. FORMAT makes the partition usable by installing the filesystem.
2. FDISK recognizes primary and extended DOS partitions.
3. An extended partition allows you to create logical drives inside the partition.
4. You boot from the active partition.

Lab Report 13.2

1. FAT and FAT32.
2. 486DX 66MHz processor.
3. Any two of the following will work: improved user interface, improved PnP support, enhanced application support, new hardware support, networking enhancements, tight Internet integration, new system tools and wizards.

Lab Report 13.3

1. FAT, FAT32 and NTFS.
2. The installation requires 650MB free; however, 1GB is recommended.
3. Makeboot.exe or makebt32.exe. Makeboot is a 16-bit application and makebt32 is the 32-bit application. You use the one that is suitable for the operating system used to create the boot disk.
4. Windows 2000 comes in four different product lines: Windows 2000 Professional, Windows 2000 Server, Windows 2000 Advanced Server, and Windows 2000 Data Center.

Lab Report 13.4

1. FAT, FAT32, and NTFS.
2. The Windows Magnifier and the Windows Narrator can be installed during the installation process.
3. Windows XP requires activation as a means to prevent software piracy. Failure to activate will cause Windows XP to shut down after 30 days.
4. Activation gathers information about the computer's hardware; it does not collect personal information.

Chapter 14

Windows Hardware Installation

LABS YOU WILL PERFORM IN THIS CHAPTER:

- ✓ Lab 14.1: Modifying Driver Signing
- ✓ Lab 14.2: Installing a Non–Plug-and-Play Device
- ✓ Lab 14.3: Installing a Plug-and-Play Device

This chapter covers how to install a device. Every device must be configured to work properly. This configuration includes installing the drivers so the device will work with the operating system. The configuration must also cover the unique hardware settings like the I/O address, IRQ, and occasionally the DMA channel.

One of the recent improvements Microsoft has introduced is *driver signing,* which ensures that device drivers function correctly with their operating systems. The additional benefit of driver signing is the assurance that the driver has not been modified since its signing. This eliminates the possibility of viruses being hidden in the driver. Because not all drivers are signed, especially older drivers, the first lab in this chapter will cover how to configure the driver signing policy.

Plug-and-Play (PnP) devices simplify this process by automatically configuring the device and then searching for the device driver. Unfortunately, not all operating systems do a good job with PnP, and not all devices are capable of allowing the operating system to perform their configuration. So, every technician needs to understand how to install a non-PnP device. The A+ exam covers the requirements to install both types of devices. This chapter will also cover how to install both types.

For more information, see Chapter 15 of David Groth's *A+ Complete Study Guide* (Sybex, 2003).

Lab 14.1: Modifying Driver Signing

Driver signing is a relatively new option designed to improve system stability. Microsoft introduced driver signing with Windows 2000. It controls the installation of new drivers; you can block, warn, or allow the installation of unsigned drivers. Unsigned drivers may have been tampered with or may cause system instability. To reduce problems, Windows 2000 and Windows XP automatically look for driver signing and then take the action you have selected. Signed drivers have been tested to verify compatibility and have not been modified by others.

Upon completion of this lab, you will be able to control driver signing.

Set Up

For this lab, you will need a computer running Windows 2000 or Windows XP.

Exercise

The driver signing options include Ignore, Warn, and Block. Blocking unsigned drivers gives you the most protection from incompatible or modified drivers. The warn option allows you to decide which drivers to install based on your opinion of the driver. You should take care when installing unsigned drivers. Ignore opens up your system to modified drivers and drivers that may cause your system to crash. This option will not check for driver signings.

1. Open Control Panel.

    In Windows 2000:

    > Start ➤ Settings ➤ Control Panel

    In Windows XP:

    > Start ➤ Control Panel

2. Open the System applet.

    In Windows 2000, double-click the System icon.

    In Windows XP:

    > Performance and Maintenance ➤ System

3. In the Systems Properties window, click on the Hardware tab.

4. Click the Driver Signing button to open the Driver Signing window. Note the default Driver Signing option:

    _____

5. Close the Driver Signing windows and the System Properties window.

Lab Report 14.1

1. What function does driver signing provide?

    _____

    _____

    _____

    _____

2. Where are the driver signing options located?

_____

_____

_____

_____

3. Which driver signing option gives you the most protection?

_____

_____

_____

_____

Lab 14.2: Installing a Non–Plug-and-Play Device

Most of the devices you will install in today's computer world are PnP compatible. However, you will still run into devices that require you to configure them to work properly in the computer.

Upon completion of this lab, you will be able to install a non-PnP device.

Set Up

For this lab, you will need the following:

- A computer running Windows 98, Windows 2000, or Windows XP
- A new device for installation
- Device driver CD or floppies
- Device documentation

Exercise

The first step in this lab is to identify which resources are available for use by the new device. This requires you to look at the IRQs, I/O addresses, and possibly DMA channels. Once you identify which resources are available, you need to look at which resources can be set on the device. You may have to disable another device for this to work. If the other device is PnP, it should be reconfigured after the non-PnP device is up and running.

1. Boot the computer. Record the system information.

    In Windows 98:

    > Start ➢ Programs ➢ Accessories ➢ System Tools ➢ System Information

    In Windows 2000:

    > Right-click on My Computer ➢ Manage

    > Computer Management window ➢ System Information ➢ Hardware Resources

    In Windows XP:

    > Start ➢ Help and Support ➢ Use Tools to View Your Computer Information and Diagnose Problems ➢ My Computer Information ➢ General System Information

2. Record which IRQs and I/O addresses are available:

    _____

    _____

3. Read the device's documentation and check which IRQs and I/O addresses are usable by the device. Decide which IRQ and I/O address you will use for the device.

4. Set the device to use the appropriate IRQ and I/O address. The documentation tells you how to set the DIP switches or position the jumpers for the settings.

5. Turn off the computer and remove the cover.

 WARNING Remember to safeguard all of your components. Follow the safety procedure listed earlier in the book for electrostatic discharge (ESD).

6. Install the new device in an empty slot. Secure the device using the installation screw.

7. Replace the cover and boot the computer.

8. Open Control Panel and double-click on the Add New Hardware icon.

9. Follow the on-screen prompts until you get to the option that asks if you want Windows to search for the new hardware. Select No, I Want to Select the Hardware from a List. Click Next.

10. From the Hardware Type list, select the type of device. Click Next.
11. Click the Have Disk option. Place the CD or floppy in the drive.
12. Follow the on-screen prompts to complete the installation.

Lab Report 14.2

1. What resources need to be configured on a non-PnP device?

_____

_____

_____

_____

2. How do you identify the available resources in a computer?

_____

_____

_____

_____

3. How is an IRQ typically set on a non-PnP device?

_____

_____

_____

_____

4. What utility allows you to add non-PnP devices?

_____

_____

_____

_____

5. What do you do if no IRQs are available for use?

_____

_____

_____

_____

Lab 14.3: Installing a Plug-and-Play Device

Most devices today support Plug and Play, which simplifies configuration. As you add or upgrade hardware with any PnP operating system, the OS should automatically recognize the device and install drivers to support the device. Most of the time, the driver you get will be adequate; however, you may still want to search the Internet for the latest and greatest driver for the device. This way you will be able to take full advantage of the device's features.

This lab has you install a new device and watch the PnP features work. You will then go into Device Manager to update the driver. If you do not have a new device to install, remove an existing device like a sound card, modem, or NIC. Once you've removed the device, boot the computer and follow any screen prompts to remove the device drivers

Upon completion of this lab, you will be able to:

- Install and configure a Plug-and-Play device
- Change a device driver

Set Up

For this lab, you will need the following:

- A computer running Windows 98, Windows 2000, or Windows XP

- A new device for installation
- Device driver CD or floppies

Exercises

Before you remove the device, make sure that you note all configuration settings for the device, including the current location of the device driver.

Installing a PnP Device

1. Turn off the computer and remove the cover.

 WARNING   Remember to safeguard all of your components. Follow the safety procedure listed earlier in the book for ESD.

2. Install the new device in an empty slot. Secure the device using the installation screw.
3. Replace the cover and boot the computer.
4. Once you have logged in, the computer should automatically detect the new device and begin searching for a suitable driver.
5. If a driver is not located on the hard drive automatically, you are requested to provide the location of a suitable driver. A window opens in which you tell the computer where to look for the driver. Put the CD or floppy in the appropriate drive and tell the computer to search for the driver on the CD or floppy drive.
6. Click Finish to complete the installation.

Changing a Device Driver

1. Open Control Panel.

   In Windows 98/2000:

   > Start ➤ Settings ➤ Control Panel

   In Windows XP:

   > Start ➤ Control Panel

2. Open the System applet.

   In Windows 98/2000, double-click the System icon.

   In Windows XP:

   > Performance and Maintenance ➤ System

3. In Windows 98, skip this step and proceed to step 4. Otherwise, click the Hardware tab.
4. Click on Device Manager.
5. Select the device you want to update or change.

New device drivers can be located on the Internet. You can either go to the Microsoft website or go directly to the manufacturer's website. Another site that is often useful for locating device drivers is www.driverguide.com.

6. Right-click on the device and select Properties.

7. Click on the Driver tab.

8. Click the Update Driver button.

9. Follow the on-screen prompts until you get to the screen that gives you an option to search for a better driver or display a list. Select the option Search for a Better Driver (the recommended option). Click Next.

10. Select the driver's location. This may be on a floppy or CD. If you downloaded a new driver, specify the location where the download was stored.

11. When the wizard locates the new driver, click Next to continue.

12. The wizard shows you what is about to be done. Click Finish to install the new driver.

Lab Report 14.3

1. Where can you locate new drivers for a device?

    _____

    _____

    _____

    _____

2. Where do you look to see the device driver that is being used for a device?

    _____

    _____

    _____

    _____

3. Why would you want to update a device driver?

_____

_____

_____

_____

Answers to Lab Reports

Lab Report 14.1

1. Driver signing is designed to help eliminate incompatible and modified drivers.
2. Driver signing options are located on the Hardware tab of the System applet in Control Panel.
3. Block.

Lab Report 14.2

1. You need to set IRQ and I/O address information. In some cases you may need to set the DMS as well.
2. Look in the system information to determine what resources are available.
3. The IRQ is typically set using jumpers or DIP switches.
4. Add New Hardware in Control Panel lets you install a new device. In Windows XP, you can add the hardware in Printers and Other Hardware.
5. You may have to disable another device. Good ones to consider are any unused serial or parallel ports.

Lab Report 14.3

1. You can locate new device drivers by searching the Internet. Good places to start are manufacturers' and Microsoft's websites.
2. You will find the device driver information on the General tab in the device properties. The device properties can be found in Device Manager.
3. To take advantage of all the features or to get a more stable version of the driver.

Chapter

15

Windows Networking

This chapter deals with how to get two or more computers to talk with each other so they can pass data between themselves. In order for the computers to communicate, they need to have a protocol. We will cover how to install and troubleshoot network protocols.

After the protocols are installed and configured, you need to create shares that contain the information you wish to allow other users to see. This process is called *sharing*. Sharing allows you to give other users access to your folders and printers. Because you may need to control who is accessing your resources, Windows XP has implemented a firewall. A *firewall* is a packet filter that helps you to control access. If you have a direct connection to the Internet, such as DSL or a cable modem, you should definitely control access to your computer.

For more information, see Chapter 16 of David Groth's *A+ Complete Study Guide* (Sybex, 2003).

Lab 15.1: Installing Network Protocols and Services

Network protocols are necessary so that two computers can communicate with each other. Many protocols have been developed by companies and organizations trying to compete in the networking market. Each organization developed its own set of rules (what many call a *language*) to allow computers pass data back and forth. The key network protocols are *Transmission Control Protocol/Internet Protocol* (TCP/IP), Internetwork Packet eXchange/Sequenced Packet eXchange (IPX/SPX), and *NetBIOS Extended User Interface* (NetBEUI).

NetBEUI was developed by IBM and adopted by Microsoft for network communications. It was originally chosen because it is a stable, fast network protocol. It requires no user configuration, which makes it very easy to use. Its simplicity makes it very fast with little network overhead. Its main limitation is that it is not routable, which means it is effective only on small networks.

Novell developed the IPX/SPX protocol for use with its NetWare server line. Many people feel that Novell wrote the book about how to do networking. The IPX/SPX protocol suite was the most widely used protocol stack until the popularity of the Internet replaced it with TCP/IP. Microsoft wrote a NetBIOS-compatible version of IPX/SPX called NWLink. IPX/SPX is a scalable network protocol that can be routed; it is still used on large and medium-sized networks.

TCP/IP was developed as part of a Department of Defense initiative that resulted in the Information Superhighway, or what we now call the Internet. The TCP/IP protocol stack is routable and can be scaled to very large networks. It is the native network protocol of many operating systems, including Unix and Linux. It has been adopted as the core protocol for operating systems such as Microsoft Windows and Novell's NetWare 5.0 and up.

Because TCP/IP is the default network protocol, we will cover how to configure it, not install it. TCP/IP requires that you configure the IP address and subnet mask. The *IP address* is a 32-bit number broken into four octets. The numbers in each octet can range from 0–255. The IP address contains two pieces of information, the network ID and the host ID. The job of the *subnet mask* is to let you know which octets belong to the network ID and which octets represent the host ID. A 255 in the subnet mask makes the corresponding octet in the IP address belong to the network ID. A 0 in the subnet mask represents the host ID in the corresponding octets of the IP address.

Additionally, TCP/IP lets you configure the default gateway, DNS addresses, and WINS addresses. The *default gateway* is the router on your network that allows you to communicate with hosts on other networks. The *DNS address* is the IP address of the server that is hosting the DNS service that resolves computer names to IP addresses. *WINS* is a similar service written by Microsoft to resolve NetBIOS names to IP addresses.

The configuration data can be entered manually, or the Dynamic Host Configuration Protocol (DHCP) can automatically assign it to a computer. DHCP uses scopes or pools of IP addresses that it assigns to any host that requests the configuration. By default, Microsoft uses DHCP to handle TCP/IP configuration. This lab will introduce you to the windows in which you can manually enter your TCP/IP address and subnet mask.

NWLink and NetBEUI must be installed on the computer before you can use these protocol stacks. NWLink automatically detects the proper network settings. You have the option of setting the internal network ID and the frame type if necessary. NetBEUI has no user configuration; it is a self-tuning protocol that automatically sets itself up when installed. The following exercises will have you install NWLink and NetBEUI. You will also learn how to configure NWLink.

Network bindings allow you to bind a protocol to a network adapter. In Windows, you can bind multiple protocols to one adapter or bind a protocol to multiple adapters. Once multiple protocols have been bound to an adapter, the bindings allow you to control which one is used first to establish a session with another computer to transfer information. You should always place the most commonly used protocol first in the list.

Upon completion of this lab, you will be able to install and configure the following network protocols: TCP/IP, NWLink, and NetBEUI.

Set Up

For this lab, you will need a working computer running Windows 98, Windows 2000, or Windows XP.

Exercises

In these exercises you will be configuring TCP/IP, installing and configuring NWLink and NetBEUI, and configuring network bindings.

Configuring TCP/IP

To configure TCP/IP,

1.   Open the Properties window of your Internet connection.

    In Windows 98:

        Start ➤ Settings ➤ Control Panel. Double-click on the Network icon.

    In Windows 2000:

        Start ➤ Settings ➤ Control Panel. Double-click on the Network and Dial-Up Connec-
        tions icon. Right-click on the icon that represents your connection to the Internet.
        Select Properties from the menu.

    In Windows XP:

        Start ➤ Control Panel ➤ Network and Internet Connections ➤ Network Connections.
        Right-click on the icon that represents your connection to the Internet. Select Proper-
        ties from the menu.

2.   In the Properties window, select the Internet Protocol (TCP/IP) or TCP/IP. Each operating
    system uses a slightly different name. Once TCP/IP is highlighted, click the Properties button.

3.   On the General tab, notice that Obtain IP Address Automatically is the default setting.
    Click the Use the Following IP Address radio button. Record the fields that now allow you
    to enter information (in Windows 98, this information is on the IP Address tab):

    _____

    _____

4.   Click on the Advanced button (this button is not available in Windows 98). Record the tabs
    that can be used to enter TCP/IP information:

    _____

    _____

5.   Click OK to close the Advanced window. Click the Obtain an IP Address Automatically
    radio button. This option has this host request its IP address information from a DHCP
    server.

6.   Click OK to close the TCP/IP Properties window. Leave the interface Properties window
    open for use in the next set of exercises.

Installing and Configuring NWLink and NetBEUI

To install and configure NWLink and NetBEUI,

1.   Click the Install or Add button from the interface Properties window.

2. Double-click on the Protocol icon to open the Protocol window.

3. Select NWLink NetBIOS Compatible Transport.

4. Click OK to close the Protocol Window. Click OK to close the interface Properties window.

Configuring Network Bindings

In Windows 98:

1. From the Network Properties window, click on the interface and click the Properties button.

2. Click on the Bindings tab. Review the Bindings.

3. Close all the windows.

   In Windows 2000/XP:

1. From the Network and Dial-Up Connections Properties window, click Advanced in the menu.

2. Click on the Advanced Options button.

3. Click on the Adapters and Bindings tab. Here you can use the arrows to control which protocols are used and which protocol is used first.

Lab Report 15.1

1. What must be configured at a minimum for TCP/IP?

   _____

   _____

   _____

   _____

2. What is DHCP used for?

   _____

   _____

   _____

   _____

3.   What can be configured in NWLink?

_____

_____

_____

_____

4.   What can be configured in NetBEUI?

_____

_____

_____

_____

5.   What do bindings affect?

_____

_____

_____

_____

Lab 15.2: Troubleshooting Network Protocols

Often you will need to verify the installation of a protocol or troubleshoot connectivity between computers. TCP/IP comes with a number of utilities to allow you to verify the configuration and troubleshoot connectivity.

This lab will cover the use of four key commands that you can use to verify configuration and troubleshoot connectivity issues. You use WINIPCFG in Windows 98 and IPCONFIG in Windows 2000/XP to display the current TCP/IP configuration. You will be able to see the IP address, subnet mask, default gateway, DNS servers, and hardware address. Additional switches or buttons allow you to release and renew the information if you are using DHCP.

The next command is PING. It is used to verify connectivity between two computers. You can use this command to isolate where a breakdown of connectivity occurs. The final command is TRACERT, which displays the path taken by a packet to get to a destination computer.

Upon completion of this lab, you will be able to:

- Use WINIPCFG or IPCONFIG to verify the TCP/IP configuration

- Use PING and TRACERT to troubleshoot the TCP/IP configuration

- Use NSLOOKUP to verify the DNS configuration

Set Up

For this lab, you will need a computer running Windows 98, Windows 2000, or Windows XP.

Exercises

In these exercises you will use the utilities WINIPCFG, IPCONFIG, PING, and TRACERT.

Using *WINIPCFG*

To use WINIPCFG,

1. Use the following sequence in Windows 98:

   Start ➢ Programs ➢ MS-DOS Prompt.

2. Type **WINIPCFG** and press Enter. Select your adapter from the drop-down list.

3. Click the More Info button.

4. Record your IP address, subnet mask, default gateway, and hardware address:

   _____

   _____

5. Record when the lease was obtained:

   _____

Lease information will appear only if you are using automatic configuration.

6. Click the Release button. Then click the Renew button.

7. Review the TCP/IP information. Is it the same? Yes No

8. Record the new lease information:

_____

9. Record the new IP address if you received one:

_____

10. Close the IP Configuration window.

Using *IPCONFIG*

To use IPCONFIG,

1. Follow this sequence in Windows 2000/XP:

    Start ➢ Run

2. Type **cmd**. Press Enter.

3. Type **ipconfig /all**. Press Enter.

4. Record your IP address, subnet mask, default gateway, and physical address:

_____

_____

5. Record when the lease was obtained:

_____

 Lease information will appear only if you are using automatic configuration.

6. Type **ipconfig /release**. Type **ipconfig /renew**. Press Enter.

7. Review the TCP/IP information. Is it the same? Yes No

8. Record the new lease information:

   _____

9. Record the new IP address if you received one:

   _____

Using *PING*

To use PING,

1. Open a command-prompt window.

   In Windows 98:

   > Start ➢ Programs ➢ MS-DOS Prompt

   In Windows 2000/XP:

   > Start ➢ Run. Type **cmd**. Press Enter.

2. Type **ping 127.0.0.1**. Press Enter to ping the loopback address. Doing so verifies whether the TCP/IP protocol stack is working properly.

3. Ping your IP address by typing **ping X.X.X.X**. Press Enter. Replace the Xs with the IP address that you recorded earlier. Doing so verifies that your network adapter is functioning properly.

4. Ping the IP address of the default gateway to verify that you have connectivity to the router.

5. Ping the IP address of a site on the Internet to verify connectivity outside of your local network.

6. Ping the name of your favorite site on the Internet to verify that DNS is working properly.

 You may not get a reply from some sites on the Internet. Many sites have disabled responding to pings as the result of the many Internet attacks in the recent years.

Using *TRACERT*

To use TRACERT,

1. From the command prompt, type **tracert X.X.X.X**. Press Enter. Replace the Xs with the IP address or name of your favorite site on the Internet.

2. Record the number of hops taken to get to the site:

_____

 You may not get a reply from some sites on the Internet. Many sites have disabled responding to TRACERT as the result of the many Internet attacks in the recent years.

Lab Report 15.2

1. What information does IPCONFIG display?

_____

_____

_____

_____

2. What does PING do?

_____

_____

_____

_____

3. How should you use PING?

_____

_____

_____

_____

4. What does the TRACERT command display?

_____

_____

_____

_____

Lab 15.3: Creating and Accessing Shares

The whole idea behind networking is to make resources such as files available to others. This process begins with sharing folders so the files contained in the folders are available to other users on the network. Both computers used need to have the same protocol installed and configured.

Accessing Internet sites is nothing more than an elaborate system of sharing files. Your Internet browser allows you to access files and then displays them in the proper format.

Upon completion of this lab, you will be able to:

- Create a share
- Access a share on another computer

Set Up

For this lab, you will need two computers networked together.

Exercises

Once you create a share on your computer, you have the opportunity to control access to the share. In Windows 98, you can apply several levels of access control: Read Only, Full, or Depends on Password. Doing so allows you to determine if users have full access or read-only access. You can also apply passwords to control the level of access.

Windows 2000 gives you more control over how users access your resources. You can apply permissions to the share that determine who has what kind of access to the resources.

Creating a Share in Windows 98

To create a share in Windows 98,

1. Double-click on My Computer on the Desktop.

2. Open the C: drive.

3. Create a new folder called Share Test.

4. Right-click on the Share Test folder and select Sharing from the menu.

5. Click the Share As radio button.

6. Enter a comment to describe the share in the Comment field.

7. Click the Depends on Password radio button.

8. Enter a password in the Read Only Password field.

9. Enter a password in the Full Access Password field.

10. Click OK to apply the share and close the window.

Creating a Share in Windows 2000/XP

To create a share in Windows 2000/XP,

1. Double-click on My Computer on the Desktop.

2. Open the C: drive.

3. Create a new folder called Share Test.

4. Right-click on the Share Test folder and select Sharing from the menu. In Windows XP, this option is Sharing and Security.

5. Click the Share This Folder radio button.

6. Enter a comment to describe the share in the Comment field.

7. Click the Permissions button.

8. Record the default groups that will have access to the share and the level of access they have:

_____

_____

9. Click OK to close the Permissions window.

10. Click OK to apply the share and close the window.

Accessing a Share

To access a share,

1. On the second computer, open the Network applet.

    In Windows 98, double-click on the Network Neighborhood icon on the Desktop.

    In Windows 2000, double-click on the My Network Places icon on the Desktop.

    In Windows XP, use this sequence:

    > Start ➢ My Network Places

2. Double-click on the icon that represents the first computer where you created the shared folder.

3. Double-click on the Share Test folder.

For a share on Windows 98, you need to enter the password for either Read Only Access or Full Access.

Lab Report 15.3

1. What level of access control can you apply to Windows 98 shares?

    _____

    _____

    _____

    _____

2. How can you control access to shared resources in Windows 98?

    _____

    _____

    _____

    _____

3. How can you control access to shared resources in Windows 2000?

_____

_____

_____

_____

4. What service needs to be installed for Windows 98 to share resources?

_____

_____

_____

_____

Lab 15.4: Configuring Firewalls in Windows XP

Firewalls provide a security blanket that prevents others from accessing your computer from the Internet. Since the advent of permanent connections to the Internet like DSL and cable modems, you need a security system that provides full-time protection. Windows XP Professional includes a personal firewall system to provide this full-time security; it is called the Internet Connection Firewall.

A firewall works by making a forward/filter decision for every IP packet that comes to the interface. The decision is based on the source or destination IP address and on the TCP or UDP port that is being used. You should use the firewall to close down any unused ports or to exclude access based on IP addresses.

Upon completion of this lab, you will be able to enable the Internet Connection Firewall.

Set Up

For this lab, you will need a computer running Windows XP.

Exercise

If you are using DSL or a cable modem, you need to know how to enable the protection of the Internet Connection Firewall provided by Microsoft. This exercise will show you how to enable it to protect your computer and data from outsiders.

1. Open the Network Connections window:

    Start ➢ Connect To ➢ Show All Connections

2. Right-click on the icon to for your Internet connection. Select Properties from the menu to open the Properties window.

3. Click on the Advanced tab. Check the Protect My Computer and Network by Limiting or Preventing Access to This Computer from the Internet option in the Internet Connection Firewall section.

4. Click OK to close the windows and complete the activation of the firewall.

Lab Report 15.4

1. What is a firewall in Windows XP?

    _____

    _____

    _____

    _____

2. Where is the firewall enabled?

    _____

    _____

    _____

    _____

3. Which Windows products are protected by Microsoft's Internet Connection Firewall?

    _____

    _____

    _____

    _____

4. On which tab on the Properties window is the Internet Connection Firewall found?

    _____

    _____

    _____

    _____

Answers to Lab Reports

Lab Report 15.1

1. You must configure the TCP/IP address and subnet mask at a minimum. This can be done automatically or manually.
2. DHCP is used to automatically configure the TCP/IP parameters.
3. NWLink allows you to configure the network address and the frame type.
4. NetBEUI has no configurable parameters.
5. Bindings control which protocols are used on an adapter and the order in which they are used.

Lab Report 15.2

1. IPCONFIG displays the TCP/IP configuration information. By using the IPCONFIG /ALL command, you can see the IP address, subnet mask, default gateway, DNS Server, WINS Server, DHCP Server, DHCP lease, and physical address.
2. PING is a utility that tests connectivity between two computers.
3. PING is used to troubleshoot where a problem with the network may lie. First ping the loopback address 127.0.0.1 to test the installation of the protocol stack. The next ping to the local address tests the NIC. The third ping to the default gateway tests local connectivity to other computers. The final ping to the other interface of the router tests the router's functionality.
4. TRACERT shows the path that a packet takes to get to a destination computer. You can use this information to determine which routers are being used and potentially locate any bottlenecks.

Lab Report 15.3

1. Read Only, Full, or Depends on Password.
2. You can control access to resources by placing a password on the share.
3. You can control access to resources by configuring the permissions to the share.
4. File and Print Sharing Services need to be installed for Windows 98 to be able to share resources.

Lab Report 15.4

1. Software that makes forward or filter decisions on packets based on IP address and port information.

2. The Internet Connection Firewall is enabled in the Properties window on the interface that connects to the Internet.

3. Windows XP comes with Microsoft's Internet Connection Firewall software.

4. The Internet Connection Firewall option is found on the Advanced tab.

Chapter

16

Windows Optimization

LABS YOU WILL PERFORM IN THIS CHAPTER:

We all want our computers to work as fast as they possibly can. As you add new software or hardware, you may want to spend some time to ensure that the components are working as best they can so the computer works at its fastest.

Throughout this book we have discussed how to upgrade components on the computer. The question that is frequently asked is which component will give the most value for the dollars spent. One of the first steps is to find out how the system is operating and determine the system bottlenecks. Lab 16.4 will show you how to monitor the system so that you can determine your system's performance. With the information you glean from this monitoring, you will be able to determine which components need to be upgraded. You will also be able to see if the upgrade had the desired effects.

The other exercises covered in this chapter are some general procedures that will help you optimize the performance of your computer.

 For more information, see Chapter 17 of David Groth's *A+ Complete Study Guide* (Sybex, 2003).

Lab 16.1: Configuring Virtual Memory

Every operating system must be able to create a temporary storage space for information. This is the responsibility of RAM. As we expect more from our computers, the demands on RAM also increase.

Memory requirements grow as the complexity of the operating system increases. To boost the amount of space that can be used for memory, the operating system allows you to use part of the hard drive as virtual memory. This area is called the *swap file* or *page file*.

Upon completion of this lab, you will be able to:

- Configure the size of the swap or page file

Set Up

You will need a working computer using Windows 98, Windows 2000, and Windows XP.

Exercises

In these exercises, we will show you how to configure virtual memory for Windows 98, Windows 2000, and Windows XP. There are many similarities in this process, but the location for the settings is different for each operating system.

Configuring the Size of the Paging/Swap File for Windows 98

1.   Open the System icon in Control Panel:

Start ➤ Settings ➤ Control Panel ➤ System

2.   On the General tab, record the amount of RAM in your system:

_____

3.   Click on the Performance tab.

4.   Click the Virtual Memory button.

5.   In the Virtual Memory window, click the Let Me Specify My Own Virtual Memory Settings option.

6.   In the Minimum field, enter the number that equals the amount of RAM. In the Maximum field, enter three times the amount of RAM.

7.   Click OK. You will receive a warning that asks you to confirm your actions. Click Yes.

8.   Click OK to close the System Properties window.

9.   Reboot the system. The new settings are now set.

10. Repeat these steps to set virtual memory back to being automatically controlled by Windows.

Configuring the Size of the Paging/Swap File for Windows 2000

1.   Open the System icon in Control Panel:

Start ➤ Settings ➤ Control Panel ➤ System

2.   On the General tab, record the amount of RAM in your system:

_____

3.   Click on the Advanced tab to access the virtual memory settings.

4.   In the Performance section, click the Performance Options button.

5.   In the Performance Options window, click the Change button in the Virtual Memory section.

6.   Note the size and location of the current page file:

_____

_____

7. In the Virtual Memory window, in the Initial size field, enter the number that equals the amount of RAM. In the Maximum field, enter three times the amount of RAM.

8. Click OK. You will receive a warning that asks you to confirm your actions. Click Yes.

9. Click OK to close the System Properties window.

10. Reboot the system. The new settings are now set.

11. Repeat these steps to set the virtual memory back to the original settings.

Configuring the Size of the Paging/Swap File for Windows XP

1. Open the System icon in Control Panel:

    Start ➤ Control Panel ➤ Performance and Maintenance ➤ System

2. On the General tab, record the amount of RAM in your system:

    _____

3. Click on the Advanced tab to access the virtual memory settings.

4. Click the Settings button in the Performance section.

5. In the Performance Options window, click on the Advanced tab and click the Change button in the Virtual Memory section.

6. Note the size and location of the current page file:

    _____

    _____

7. In the Virtual Memory window, first click Custom and then in the Initial size field enter the number that equals 1.5 times the amount of RAM. In the Maximum size field, enter three times the amount of RAM.

8. Click OK. You will receive a warning that asks you to confirm your actions. Click Yes.

9. Click OK to close the System Properties window.

10. Reboot the system. The new settings are now set.

11. Repeat these steps to set the virtual memory back to the original settings.

Lab Report 16.1

1. What is virtual memory?

_____

_____

_____

_____

2. How much virtual memory should you use?

_____

_____

_____

_____

3. What is the name of the file used in Windows 98?

_____

_____

_____

_____

4. What is the name of the file used in Windows 2000 and Windows XP?

_____

_____

_____

Lab 16.2: Configuring Caching

Cache is a term that describes a type of memory space used to store frequently used data. The first Microsoft caching program was SMARTDRV. This was replaced by VCACHE in Windows 98. Windows NT has its own programs to handle caching. When the computer is operating efficiently, the majority of information needed by the user and the processor is located in cache. When data is written or read from the main memory, a copy is placed into cache with the main memory address. Cache then monitors subsequent reads to see if the data is already in cache. If the data is in cache, then a cache hit is recorded and the main memory read is aborted. If the data is not in cache, then it is fetched from the main memory. If cache is not configured properly, then the system wastes a lot of CPU cycles retrieving needed data.

Upon completion of this lab, you will be able to configure caching for Windows 98, Windows 2000, and Windows XP.

Set Up

For this lab, you will need a computer running Windows 98 and a computer running Windows 2000 or Windows XP.

Exercises

You must take care when configuring cache in any Windows environment. The configuration requires that you alter either the system.ini file for Windows 98 or the Registry for Windows 2000/XP. A mistake in these settings can cause the system to become unbootable. The right setting, however, can improve system performance by allowing the system to use part of your RAM as cache.

In Windows 98, do not use SMARTDRV. Windows 98 uses VCACHE, a routine that is an improvement of SMARTDRV; if you use SMARTDRV, the two will conflict with each other and decrease performance.

Configuring *VCACHE*

1. Right-click on My Computer and select Properties. Record the amount of RAM in your system. Then close the System Properties window.

_____

_____

2. Right-click on My Computer and select Explore from the menu.

3. Navigate to the `Windows` directory.

4. In the `Windows` directory, locate the `system.ini` file. Right-click on it and select Open from the menu. Doing so opens the `system.ini` file in Notepad.

5. Locate the section labeled `[vcache]`.

6. Locate the entry `MinFileCache=`. Change the value based on Table 16.1.

7. Locate the entry `MaxFileCache=`. Change the value based on Table 16.1.

 You may have to type the entries into the `system.ini` file. Type them exactly as shown in steps 6 and 7.

TABLE 16.1   System.ini VCACHE Values

RAM	MinFileCache	MaxFileCache
16MB	1024	4096
16MB–32MB	2048	8192
32MB–64MB	8192	16384
> 64MB–128MB	16384	32768
> 128MB	32768	65536

8. Save the file and close it. Reboot the system for the changes to take effect.

Setting Cache Setting in the Registry

1. In Windows 2000 or Windows XP, from the Run command, type **regedt32**.

2. When the Registry Editor opens, navigate to the Memory Management key:

    `HKey_Local_Machine\System\CurrentControlSet\Control\Session Manager\Memory Management`

3. Locate the value `LargeSystemCache`. Double-click to open it for editing.

4. Change the Data field value to 1 if it is not already set. This value turns on the Large System Cache function that allows the operating system to use all unused RAM as cache.

5. Reboot the system for the changes to take effect.

Lab Report 16.2

1. What is cache?

   _____

   _____

   _____

   _____

2. What manages cache in Windows 98?

   _____

   _____

   _____

3. How do you set the values for VCACHE in Windows 98?

   _____

   _____

   _____

4. Where do you set the Large System Cache in Windows 2000?

   _____

   _____

   _____

   _____

Lab 16.3: Defragmenting the Hard Drive

Computers can have many problems that grow over time, including the fragmentation of files. When you create a file, it normally occupies contiguous hard-drive space (the clusters used to store the file are adjacent to each other). Over time, as the file size increases, there may not be enough contiguous space for the file. So, the file gets broken up. This process is called *fragmentation*. When enough files become fragmented, the hard drive wastes time going to different clusters to retrieve them. If fragmentation becomes bad enough, a condition called *disk thrashing* occurs: Operations slow noticeably, and the hard-drive light flickers to indicate constant activity.

Microsoft provides a utility called Disk Defragmenter to help the hard drive reorganize itself. *Defragmentation* is a process of rewriting files and organizing them so that access to the files is improved. This process can take several hours if you do not have adequate free space for the system to rewrite files or if there is a lot of fragmentation on the hard drive.

Disk Defragmenter is a utility that improves performance of the hard drive. You may want to run this utility on a regular basis. Because it can take several hours to complete, and because it is a good idea not to have any thing else running at the same time, you may want to have Disk Defragmenter run after you go to bed. If any files are open or in use they cannot be defragmented. A good practice is to review the report that is generated at the end of the process to see if any files were not defragmented. The process is the same for all Windows operating systems; only the location of the utility varies.

Upon completion of this lab, you will be able to:

- Defragment a partition on a hard drive

Set Up

You will need a computer running Windows 98, Windows 2000, or Windows XP.

Exercise

To run Disk Defragmenter,

1. Close all programs.
2. Launch the Disk Defragmenter utility.

   In Windows 98:

   > Start ➢ Programs ➢ Accessories ➢ System Tools ➢ Disk Defragmenter

   In Windows 2000:

   > Start ➢ Programs ➢ Accessories ➢ System Tools ➢ Disk Defragmenter

   In Windows XP:

   > Start ➢ All Programs ➢ Accessories ➢ System Tools ➢ Disk Defragmenter

3. Select the drive you want defragmented. Click **OK** in Windows 98; click Defragment in Windows 2000/XP.

4. The system displays a summary of the progress being made as it defragments the drive.

5. Once the process is complete, click View Report to see the details. Note which files (if any) Disk Defragmenter was not able to defragment.

 Windows 2000/XP give you an additional option: Analyze. This option analyzes the partition to see whether you need to run the defragmentation process.

6. Close the Defragmenter window.

Lab Report 16.3

1. What is a fragmented file?

_____

_____

_____

_____

2. Why should you run Disk Defragmenter?

_____

_____

_____

_____

3. What does the Analyze button do in Windows 2000 and Windows XP?

_____

_____

_____

_____

4. What is one reason why a file may still be fragmented after you run Disk Defragmenter?

_____

_____

_____

_____

Lab 16.4: Using System Monitor

The first step in optimizing any system is to determine what is currently happening in the system. Many people want to improve performance, and they often waste money by upgrading components that are not currently causing a system bottleneck. A *system bottleneck* is a component that is causing the overall system to slow down.

Microsoft provides the System Monitor utility, which can help you see how well your components are performing. By analyzing performance, you can determine which components need to be upgraded. You should start your analysis by looking at the major components: CPU, RAM, and hard drive. From there, you can expand your examination by evaluating the network and other devices that make up your system.

System Monitor is installed by default in Windows 2000 and Windows XP. You have to install System Monitor in Windows 98.

Upon completion of this lab, you will be able to:

-   Install System Monitor in Windows 98
-   View performance activity on a Windows 98/2000/XP computer

Set Up

For this lab, you will need a computer running Windows 98, Windows 2000, or Windows XP. You will need the Windows 98 Installation CD to install System Monitor.

Exercises

In this set of exercises, you will look at CPU, RAM, and hard-drive performance on a computer. The first step in Windows 98 is to install System Monitor; the utility also works differently in Windows 98. In Windows 2000/XP, the difference is in the way you launch the utility.

Installing System Monitor in Windows 98

1. Open Add/Remove Programs in Control Panel:

    Start ➤ Settings ➤ Control Panel ➤ Add/Remove Programs
2. Click on the Windows Setup tab to open the Windows Setup dialog box.
3. Highlight System Tools and click Details.

 Be careful not to click the check box. Doing so installs all the system tools.

---

4. Click the System Monitor check box and then click OK.
5. Click OK in the Add/Remove Programs Properties window.
6. When prompted, insert the CD into the CD-ROM drive. Click OK to install the files.
7. Close Control Panel.

Viewing Performance Activity in Windows 98

In Windows 98,

1. Open System Monitor:

    Start ➤ Programs ➤ Accessories ➤ System Tools ➤ System Monitor
2. When the System Monitor opens, it shows the Kernel category with the Processor Usage (%) item active. By default, it collects information every 5 seconds. You will add some items in different categories by using the Edit menu. (There are icons to accomplish the same tasks; hover your mouse over the icons so you can see what they do.) Choose this menu item:

    Edit ➤ Add Item
3. Under Category, click Memory Manager. This option allows you to add items related to memory. Click Allocated Memory.
4. Click the Explain button. Doing so provides an explanation about the item. Click OK.

5. Click OK to add allocated memory.

6. View the graph of allocated memory.

7. Add an item to view the number of reads per second from the hard drive:

> Edit ➤ Add Item ➤ File System ➤ Reads/Second

8. Add an item to view the number of cache hits:

> Edit ➤ Add Item ➤ Disk Cache ➤ Cache Hits

9. Add an item to view the number of threads:

> Edit ➤ Add Item ➤ Kernel ➤ Threads

10. Add an item to view the size of the disk cache:

> Edit ➤ Add Item ➤ Memory Manager ➤ Disk Cache Size

11. View System Monitor for a couple of minutes. Record the peak values for the items:

_____

_____

_____

_____

12. Launch an application.

13. View System Monitor for a couple of minutes. Record the new peak values for the items:

_____

_____

_____

_____

14. Create a snapshot of the activity:

> File ➤ Start Logging

15. Accept the default log name by clicking Save.

16. After a few minutes, stop the logging activity:

> File ➤ Stop Logging

17. Close System Monitor.

Viewing Performance Activity in Windows 2000 and Windows XP

To view performance activity in Window 2000 and Windows XP,

1. Open the Performance window.

   In Windows 2000:

   > Start ➤ Settings ➤ Control Panel ➤ Administrative Tools ➤ Performance

   In Windows XP:

   > Start ➤ Control Panel ➤ Performance and Maintenance ➤ Administrative Tools ➤ Performance

2. To see any activity, you must add counters to the window. To add counters, click the Add button in the Performance window. The Add button looks like a plus sign.

3. In the Add Counters window, click on the Performance Object drop-down menu and select the Processor object. Highlight the % Processor Time counter in the Select Counter from List field. Click Add.

4. Click on the Performance Object drop-down menu and select the Memory object. Highlight the Pages/sec counter in the Select Counter from List field. Click Add.

5. Click on the Performance Object drop-down menu and select the Paging File object. Highlight the %Usage counter in the Select Counter from List field. Click Add.

6. Click on the Performance Object drop-down menu and select the Physical Disk object. Highlight the Disk Read Bytes/sec counter in the Select Counter from List field. Click Add.

7. Click Close to view the chart.

8. View System Monitor for a couple of minutes. Record the peak values for the counters:

   _____

   _____

   _____

   _____

9. Close the Performance window.

Lab Report 16.4

1. What is a system bottleneck?

_____

_____

_____

_____

2. How do you measure computer activity?

_____

_____

_____

_____

3. In Windows 2000, which object lets you look at the performance of the swap file?

_____

_____

_____

_____

4. Which counter in the Processor Performance object shows you the overall activity of the CPU?

_____

_____

_____

_____

Answers to Lab Reports

Lab Report 16.1

1. Virtual memory is space on the hard drive that is allocated for use by memory.
2. The minimum amount of virtual memory is the size of your RAM. It is recommended that the size be 1.5 to 2 times the amount of RAM for most operating systems.
3. The virtual memory file is `win386.swp` in Windows 98.
4. The virtual memory file is `pagefile.sys` in Windows 2000 and Windows XP.

Lab Report 16.2

1. Cache is part of the RAM used to store frequently accessed data.
2. VCACHE manages cache in Windows 98.
3. VCACHE settings are made in the `system.ini` file.
4. You turn on `LargeSystemCache` in the Registry.

Lab Report 16.3

1. A file becomes fragmented when it no longer occupies contiguous disk space.
2. Disk Defragmenter helps to optimize hard-drive activity by reorganizing and rewriting the data on your hard drive so that the files occupy contiguous clusters.
3. The Analyze button allows you to perform a check to see whether the partition contains fragmented files.
4. A file may still be fragmented after you run Disk Defragmenter if the file was in use or the system could not get exclusive access to the file. To prevent this from happening, you should close all programs before using Disk Defragmenter.

Lab Report 16.4

1. A system bottleneck is a component that is causing degradation of system performance. Although you will never eliminate all the bottlenecks, you can maximize performance based on your budget by identifying the slowest component.
2. Computer activity is measured using items and counters related to a category or performance object.
3. The Paging File object.
4. %ProcessorTime.

Chapter 17

Windows and Application Troubleshooting

LABS YOU WILL PERFORM IN THIS CHAPTER:

Troubleshooting is a skill that requires you to collect the required information about what is happening on your computer. Microsoft has provided you with several tools that have been bundled with their Windows family of products. In this chapter, you will learn how to collect information so that you will know where to start when troubleshooting your system. These tools, when used properly, will help you collect information that then can be used to troubleshoot what the root problem is.

For more information, see Chapter 18 of David Groth's *A+ Complete Study Guide* (Sybex, 2003).

Lab 17.1: Using Event Viewer

One of the hardest problems when troubleshooting computers is getting information from users about what has been occurring on the computer. With Windows NT, Microsoft introduced a tool to help track what has been going on. This tool is Event Viewer. By default, Event Viewer has three different log files: one for the systems, one for applications, and one for security. Most system error messages get recorded in the system log. So, when you need to get an error message from the end user, you can now get that information from Event Viewer.

Upon completion of this lab, you will be able to:

- Open Event Viewer and review the log files

Set Up

For this lab, you will need a computer running Windows 2000 or XP.

Exercise

You can easily access Event Viewer from either the Administrative Tools or from Computer Management. It should be one of the first places you look when you start to troubleshoot a system. Remember that most computer problems begin with a single problem and then cascade into a multitude of problems. Normally, when you solve the root problem, the rest disappear. Occasionally you may have multiple problems that require many troubleshooting steps.

In Event Viewer are three types of system log events—Information, Warning, and Error:

- Information events are normal events that indicate the starting and stopping of services or drivers. They are indicated by a blue *i*.

- Warning events are logged to indicate a source of future problems such as a nearly full hard drive. Warnings are indicated by an exclamation point in a yellow triangle.

- An error is recorded when a service or driver fails. An X in a red circle indicates an error.

Identifying System Events

To identify system events,

1. Open Event Viewer:

   In Windows 2000:

   > Start ➤ Settings ➤ Control Panel ➤ Administrative Tools ➤ Event Viewer

   In Windows XP:

   > Start ➤ Control Panel ➤ Performance and Maintenance ➤ Administrative Tools ➤ Event Viewer

2. Open the System Log.

3. Look at the entries.

4. Double-click on an Information entry to get the full details. Record the details.

   _____

   _____

5. Double-click on a Warning entry to get the full details. Record the information.

   _____

   _____

6. Close the Event Viewer Window.

Lab Report 17.1

1. What are the three event logs by default in Windows 2000 and Windows XP?

   _____

   _____

   _____

2. What type of information is collected in the System Event log?

    _____

    _____

    _____

    _____

3. What type of information is logged as an Information event?

    _____

    _____

    _____

    _____

4. What symbol is used for errors?

    _____

    _____

    _____

    _____

Lab 17.2: Using Dr. Watson

One of the promises Microsoft made to its end users was that Windows would become a stable platform—that is, applications would stop crashing. Even though applications still crash occasionally, Microsoft has provided a tool to help application programmers collect debugging information. This tool is Dr. Watson. Dr. Watson allows you to gather necessary information that can then be sent to the application developers so they can isolate the causes of application errors. In Windows 98, you can create a snapshot of what is running on the system at the time of the snapshot.

Upon completion of this lab, you will be able to:

- Launch Dr. Watson
- Create a snapshot in Windows 98
- Configure Dr. Watson

Set Up

For this lab, you will need a computer running Windows 98, Windows 2000, or Windows XP.

Exercises

When an application crashes constantly, you may want to collect information to send back to the developers so they can resolve the issues. The information is collected into a *dump file*. The dump file contains the data stored in memory for evaluation. This information can then be debugged to isolate which part of the code is the culprit. Often, a patch can be written to resolve all the issues.

Launching Dr. Watson

To launch Dr. Watson,

1. Choose Start ➢ Run.
2. In Windows 98, type `C:\windows\drwatson`.

   In Windows 2000/XP, type `drwtsn32`.

Creating a Snapshot in Windows 98

To create a snapshot in Windows 98,

1. Right-click on the Dr. Watson icon in the Taskbar. From the shortcut menu, select Dr Watson to collect the snapshot.
2. To view the snapshot, follow this sequence from the menu:

   View ➢ Advanced View
3. Click on the System tab and record the system information:

   _____

   _____

4. Click on the User Drivers tab and record the drivers being used by the user:

   _____

   _____

5. Click on the MS-DOS Drivers tab and record the drivers being used by DOS:

_____

_____

Configuring Dr. Watson

In Windows 98:

1. Right-click on the Dr. Watson icon on the Taskbar and select Options.

2. When the Dr. Watson Options window appears, record the number of instructions to be recorded and the dump file's path:

_____

_____

In Windows 2000 and XP:

1. After you type **drwtsn32** in the Run field, the Dr. Watson Option window opens. Record the number of instructions to be recorded and the dump file's path:

_____

_____

Lab Report 17.2

1. What type of information does Dr. Watson record?

_____

_____

_____

_____

2. How do you create a snapshot?

_____

_____

_____

_____

3. What is a dump file?

_____

_____

_____

_____

4. What options can you configure for Dr. Watson in Windows 98?

_____

_____

_____

_____

Lab 17.3: Using ScanDisk or Check Disk

ScanDisk is a utility that checks the disk surface and the files and folders on the hard drive in Windows 98. It automatically runs after the system has been improperly shut down. To prevent ScanDisk from running automatically after you start the system, you need to gracefully or properly shut down the system using one of various methods. Windows 2000 and Windows XP have a similar utility called Check Disk.

Upon completion of this lab, you will be able to:

- Run ScanDisk

Set Up

For this lab, you will need a computer running Windows 98, Windows 2000, or Windows XP.

Exercise

ScanDisk can perform two different scans, Standard and Thorough. The Standard scan just check files and folders. The Thorough Scan checks the disk surface as well. In the Advanced Options, you can select what to display, how to log, what to check for, and how to fix problems. Check Disk is used in Windows 2000 and Windows XP to automatically fix file system errors and to scan for and attempt recovery of bad sectors.

1. Open the ScanDisk or Check Disk program.

    In Windows 98:

    > In the Run command field, type **scandisk**.

    In Windows 2000:

    > Open My Computer, Right-click on the C: drive and select **Properties**. When the Properties dialog box opens, click on the **Tools** tab. From the Tools tab click on **Error-checking**.

2. When the ScanDisk or Check Disk window opens, select the drive to be scanned. Select Standard for the type of scan to be performed. Click Start.

3. When the ScanDisk Results window appears, record the number of folders, hidden files, and user files found:

    _____

    _____

4. Click Close to close the ScanDisk Results window.

5. Click the Advanced button. This option is only available with ScanDisk.

6. Note the settings used by default:

    _____

    _____

7. Close all the windows.

Lab Report 17.3

1. What tasks does ScanDisk accomplish?

_____

_____

_____

_____

2. If you lose power to the computer, why does ScanDisk automatically run?

_____

_____

_____

_____

3. What is the difference between a Standard and a Thorough scan?

_____

_____

_____

_____

4. Before you scan, what options can you select?

_____

_____

_____

Lab 17.4: Using *MSCONFIG*

MSCONFIG is a Windows 98 troubleshooting tool. It helps automate the routine troubleshooting steps that are used to fix the system configuration files. The system configuration files include the CONFIG.SYS, AUTOEXEC.BAT, SYSTEM.INI, and WIN.INI files. This tool gives you the ability to modify the system configuration files using check boxes instead of typing in the actual files using Notepad or another editing tool. This way, you can step through the file until you locate the bad line of code. The utility creates a backup of these key files and restores them after you finish.

Upon completion of this lab, you will be able to:

- Use MSCONFIG to edit key system configuration files

Set Up

For this lab, you will need a computer running Windows 98.

Exercise

In this exercise, you we will open the MSCONFIG utility and view the content of the files. The exam is only concerned with your knowing which files can be altered using this utility.

1. In the Run command field, type **msconfig**.

2. When the System Configuration Utility window opens, note the Startup Selection Options:

    _____

    _____

3. Click the Create Backup button.

4. When the Create Backup window opens, click OK to acknowledge that the backup is complete.

5. Click on the tabs. Notice that each file is opened. Each line in the file has a check box that allows you to comment out the line for the next reboot. If you were using Notepad or another editor, you could manually comment out the line by typing a semicolon before it.

6. Click the View menu item. Note the other utilities and settings you can access.

    _____

    _____

7. Close the System Configuration Utility window.

Lab Report 17.4

1. Which key system configuration files are opened using MSCONFIG?

   _____

   _____

   _____

   _____

2. How are the files modified?

   _____

   _____

   _____

   _____

3. What other utilities can be accessed from MSCONFIG?

   _____

   _____

   _____

   _____

4. What is the first step that you should do before modifying any of the system configuration files?

   _____

   _____

   _____

   _____

Answers to Lab Reports

Lab 17.1

1. The three logs are System, Application, and Security.
2. The System log is used to record information that pertains to the operating system, such as the starting and stopping of services and drivers.
3. Information events are normal to operations and are logged for information purposes.
4. A red circle with an X inside it.

Answers to Lab Report 17.2

1. Application debug information.
2. Right-click on the Dr. Watson icon in Taskbar and select Dr. Watson from the menu.
3. A dump file contains application debugging information.
4. You can configure the number of logs maintained, the file location, the number of instructions to include, and the number of stack frames to include.

Answers to Lab Report 17.3

1. ScanDisk can check for surface errors and file and folder errors.
2. ScanDisk automatically runs in case of errors caused by the sudden loss of power to the hard drive. It runs to try to correct the errors if it can, to prevent loss of data.
3. A Standard scan checks for file and folder errors. A Thorough scan adds a check of the disk surface.
4. You need to select which drive to scan and then the type of scan to be performed

Answers to Lab Report 17.4

1. The CONFIG.SYS, AUTOEXEC.BAT, SYSTEM.INI, and WIN.INI files.
2. You have the option to select or unselect each line of the system configuration file to determine which lines will be used on the next reboot.
3. You can access Device Manager, the Printers folder, display settings, multimedia settings, and the Fonts folder by clicking View in the menu.
4. Back up the files by clicking the Backup button.

Index

Note to the Reader: Throughout this index **boldfaced** page numbers indicate primary discussions of a topic. *Italicized* page numbers indicate illustrations.

N

O

T

Complete A+ Coverage

*A*ll Sybex A+ products cover both the Core Hardware and Operating System Technologies exams and have been updated based on CompTIA's 2003 exam objectives. Sybex A+ Study Guides are reviewed and approved as CompTIA Approved Quality Curriculum (CAQC).

A+® Complete Study Guide, 3rd Edition
By David Groth • ISBN: 0-7821-4243-5 • US $49.99

This Study Guide covers both exams in a single, well-organized volume. The companion CD contains an advanced testing engine with adaptive testing capabilities, four bonus exams, electronic flashcards for PCs and Palm devices, and the complete book in PDF.

A+® Complete Study Guide, Deluxe Edition
By David Groth • ISBN: 0-7821-4244-3 • US $59.99

The most comprehensive courseware available, this Deluxe Edition contains bonus CD that has instructional video footage of key hands-on procedures plus six bonus exams. The standard CD contains an advanced testing engine with adaptive testing capabilities, six bonus exams, electronic flashcards for PCs and Palm devices, and the complete book in PDF.

A+® Complete Lab Manual, 3rd Edition
By Donald R. Evans, Scott Johnson • ISBN: 0-7821-4251-6 • US $24.99

This student workbook provides a full set of lab exercises to supplement the A+ Complete Study Guide, 3rd Edition, serving as the perfect companion.

A+® Fast Pass
By David Groth • ISBN: 0-7821-4259-1 • US $29.99

This book is organized by objectives for quick review and reinforcement of chief topics. It gives you the most comprehensive set of study review features, including ten chapter review tests, two bonus exams, two sets of Flashcard exams, and a searchable Key Term Database on CD-ROM. This adds up to 500 practice questions in all.

SYBEX®

www.sybex.com

TELL US WHAT YOU THINK!

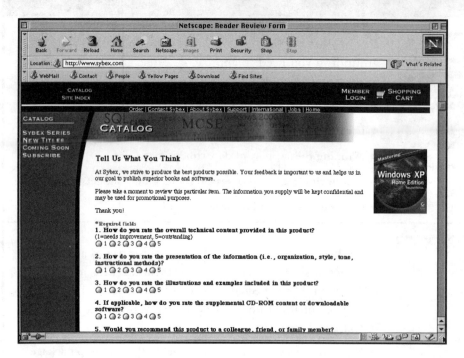

Your feedback is critical to our efforts to provide you with the best books and software on the market. Tell us what you think about the products you've purchased. It's simple:

1. Go to the Sybex website.
2. Find your book by typing the ISBN or title into the Search field.
3. Click on the book title when it appears.
4. Click **Submit a Review.**
5. Fill out the questionnaire and comments.
6. Click **Submit.**

With your feedback, we can continue to publish the highest quality computer books and software products that today's busy IT professionals deserve.

www.sybex.com

SYBEX Inc. • 1151 Marina Village Parkway, Alameda, CA 94501 • 510-523-8233